Puppet on a String

Puppet on a String

by

Helena Wilkinson

HODDER AND STOUGHTON
LONDON SYDNEY AUCKLAND TORONTO

Unless stated otherwise, all quotations are from the Good News Bible.

British Library Cataloguing in Publication Data

Wilkinson, Helena
   Puppet on a string.——(Hodder Christian
paperbacks)
   1. Anorexia nervosa——Patients——Biography
   I. Title   II. Series
   616.85'2   RC552.A5

   ISBN 0 340 34656 6

Hodder and Stoughton Editorial Office: 47 Bedford Square, London WC1E 3DP.

To my family

in memory of my much loved cousin

Kathie

who died just after this book

had been delivered to the publishers

Contents

Puppet on a String

From everyone around
There's hardly a sound,
As she fades away
Day after day,
Until painfully thin,
No more than bones and skin.

Life vanishing fast,
She's fled her cast
And stands in solitude
Letting no one intrude.
In a world of her own
No happiness is sown.

Pitiful and dejected
Is the image she's reflected,
Tearful and drooping,
She's a puppet on a string
And her last thread
Is between the living and the dead.

1

The source of life

New life bursts forth into stream,
A rising sun of golden light
Sets the delicate new scene.

Slowly it starts the course
Towards the vulnerable sea;
Flowing onward from its source.

Good and bad are seen in every part,
But to find beauty beneath the sea
In the underwater world, thrills my heart.

I made a very hurried entry into the world. The gynaecologist who was supposed to be present at the birth had not even reached the labour room in time to see me arrive! The midwife seized me and desperately tried to unravel the umbilical cord that was tied several times round my neck and twisted in and out. Anxiously she tried to prevent it from strangling me. Her face hot and bothered and her glasses steamed up – she managed it.

All the routine procedures of cleaning the baby, making sure I was breathing properly and checking my weight took place. I was a mere five pounds seven ounces and in England would have been treated as premature, but was far from being so in Africa.

There was no early contact with my mother. I was shown to her, then placed in a cot at the end of a separate ward. Babies in Africa, at that time, were made to sleep through the night and were not fed, regardless of their weight.

Whilst in hospital for the first week, the only period during the day at which my mother could make contact with me was feeding time. There was no chance for mother and child to establish a warm relationship, for the mother to cuddle her newly-born baby. Even during the short time I was feeding there was continuous noise and cigarette smoke from the visitors – the two in the evening coincided. Feeding was a very tense time.

At the end of our stay, my father came to pick us up from the Princess Elizabeth Hospital in Nairobi, the capital of Kenya. With him were my older sister, Ruth, who was nearly three, and our Goan nanny, Agnes. They were delighted with the new addition to the family and their excitement mounted as the car wound its way up the long steep hill and down again through the shady eucalyptus trees to Muguga.

My father was a forest entomologist. We lived on the edge of a research station, in an attractive bungalow which looked out over the forest to the distant blue ridge of the Ngong hills. The garden was a landscape of its own. Its valley, outdoor theatre and fascinating collection of magnificent rocks and cacti contrasted with the cascades of riotous colour of the bougainvillea on the house and the sweet fragrance of the lily garden.

At the back of our bungalow was a lovely nursery, which Ruth and I were to share. She had a bed by one window surrounded by all her zoo animals, whilst my Moses basket was placed in the big cot at the other end, with pretty posters on the wall.

Ruth was happy to have "her baby" in the nursery with her, but the novelty soon wore off when I cried throughout each night. I screamed so much that I ended up sleeping in the pram in my parents' room, so that I could be rocked and wheeled around. My mother tried cuddling me, but still I cried. Nothing would comfort me for long. After many nights, the doctor came out from Nairobi, and strode up and down the room taking ages to come to the point that he wanted me to go back into hospital.

Soon afterwards I was taken to the children's hospital and sedated with chloral. My mother came in every day to feed me and after about a week I was allowed back home again. It was only a matter of days after leaving the hospital that I developed terrible diarrhoea, particularly at night. This immediately disturbed the sleeping pattern once more and I was taken back into the children's hospital in Nairobi. By this time I was on lactogen baby food made with water. After a short spell, the diarrhoea cleared up and when the doctor was sure that the condition was completely better I was taken back home. Once we were back in Muguga the complaint started again. I was taken back into the hospital where my mother queried whether the complaint could have any connection with the borehole water which we used in Muguga. This was found to be so. Some of the minerals contained in it affected me adversely.

Apart from the very disturbed sleeping pattern at night and the tendency to be very startled and frightened if woken up during the day, I was a perfectly normal and very happy baby, especially when with other people. My development was normal and fast in spite of being a little underweight. Feeding was no problem: I happily drank one and a half bottles at a time, yearning for more in order to catch up.

I was acutely aware of sound but my mother was convinced I could not see her. She had commented about this earlier when I appeared to be very sensitive to bright light. Everyone else denied the fact, suggesting that it was probably just late development in focusing.

My mother took me along to the King George VI Hospital where, thanks to Dr Beryl Lake (later to become my godmother), it was discovered that I had severe nystagmus, being unable to focus. An appointment was made to see the eye specialist within the same hospital, who confirmed the diagnosis and wanted some investigations of the optic nerve carried out under anaesthetic. He suggested that as we were shortly going back to England to live this should be done by a Harley Street specialist.

The early stages of noticing objects and in particular the expressions on people's faces, such as a smile portraying happiness, must be very important in early life. A baby's conversation is through its response to facial expression. A baby without sight must surely feel frustrated, scared and lonely. These must have been my feelings at such an early and vulnerable stage in life.

On Palm Sunday, March 22nd 1964, I was baptised from the director's rosebowl in a little church on the research station at Muguga. It was a great excitement for everyone present as it was the first baptism in a new church which my parents had helped to build.

On Good Friday the family took up residence in one of the cottages in Muguga House so that my father could pack up the contents of our house. Just under two weeks later we caught the night train to Mombasa, arriving at the Two Fishes Hotel, Diani Beach, run by two lovely people, Beth and Allan Fish. Beth and Allan had no children of their own, but had created a hotel which was a paradise for children, amongst shady casuarina and palm trees at the edge of the tropical blue sea with its multi-coloured fish and white surf. Ruth loved the expanse of beach with its white sandcastles and the fun of the leaping waves; I was content to kick on the soft, warm sand in the shade of the casuarina trees. Beth and I seemed to have an immediate bond of love. Here with the rhythmic sound of surf in my ears, I slept through the night for the first time in my life.

In April 1964 we moved back to England for good, Ruth aged three and a half and me aged seven months. The white sandy beaches, palm trees and crystal-clear water with the mysterious East African sunsets over the hills faded into the distance, no longer a reality but a fairytale memory. After a long delay at the airport and travelling four thousand miles, the plane landed in England at midnight. We took delivery of our new car and drove through the darkness of the night a further one hundred miles to Suffolk to stay with my mother's parents, arriving at a very unsociable hour in the morning.

For the following eight months we did not have a house of our own and for the majority of the time lived with Ruth's and my godparents, staying sometimes with relatives, and taking a holiday in a little picturesque cottage in Southwold on the Suffolk coast.

Not long after we had come to England I was taken to the Moorfields Hospital in London to see the eye specialist. I was given the pre-med and left in the carrycot with my father standing by me whilst my mother went to have her eyes checked downstairs. When she came back I was screaming and obviously very frightened; immediately she picked me up and walked along the corridor whereupon I fell asleep. No sooner was I asleep in her arms than I was woken up for the anaesthetic. From that day on for many months it took two hours of gentle soothing to get me to sleep. I was forcing myself to keep my eyes open – I dared not go to sleep.

A month later I went back to Moorfields Hospital for three days of investigations. My mother mentioned to the sister that ever since the last anaesthetic I had fought sleep. Her reply was, "That sometimes happens with anaesthetics, especially with babies; it could be worse after this time." It was – I woke every hour of the night for most of the hour, so much that my mother had to take me into her room as she no longer had the energy to keep walking along the corridor.

Hospitalisation does have an effect on the child that it is apt to feel later on in life. As Rudolph Schaffer in his book *Mothering* states:

> When we turn to the immediate effects of a child's separation from his mother the picture is much clearer. A young child is likely to experience severance of the bond with his mother as devastating, if, that is, the separation occurs under traumatic circumstances and the child is sent to a strange environment and is there looked after by strangers, as happens, for instance, in hospitalisation or admission to public care.

As it is stipulated that separation before the age of seven months is of little consequence and most of my hospitalisation was before this age, I thought that it could bear no relation to what happened to me later. However, my concept changed when Rudolph Schaffer went on to say:

> In the past, separation studies have exclusively concentrated on relatively gross indignities such as crying, changes in activity, and sleeping or eating disorders. But in view of the fine synchronisation

established between mother and baby from the early weeks on, we ought to consider the possibility that at a much more microscopic level interaction processes can also be disrupted before seven months. Even if the infant reveals no awareness of the mother's absence and therefore shows no separation upset, might not established synchronisation patterns be distorted when someone else takes the mother's place – someone who has not learned the specific characteristics of that particular infant, who may not have the motivation to be as sensitive to his signals as his mother, and whose own behaviour in interaction may be entirely different? If this were the case, some sort of effect would register in the infant's behaviour, though the indications might well be far more subtle than those in separated infants beyond the seven months' milestone.

By Christmas my father had been offered a job with ICI and we moved into a house in Berkshire, situated in a quiet cul-de-sac within walking distance of the town. The house, a chalet-bungalow, was new, and the garden, like our Kenya one, needed to be made, so once again my parents set about creating a home and garden of beauty for us.

I was a bundle of energy; climbing, running and playing. At the age of two I was sent to playschool, which I absolutely adored. There were no problems over being separated from my parents: no sooner had I arrived than I was on the swings or splashing around with the paint. I enjoyed every minute of my time there. Then I began to get very bad earache. I remember many a night sleeping with my ear pressed to a hot water-bottle covered with a jumper or a vest. The doctor decided that when I was three my tonsils ought to be removed. Once more the anaesthetic upset me. Apparently I was like a wild tiger when I was trying to fight the dizzy feeling.

I began school at the age of four, at a local infant school. Although very shy, I did not take long to settle and started to enjoy myself almost immediately. My memories are mostly of the art and craft lessons and the big gymnasium full of exciting equipment. Later that year, when I was five, I taught myself to roller-skate. I would spend hours speeding up and down the path, making up dances and generally amusing myself.

Just before I was due to start junior school we went on holiday to Ibiza. Here the days were full of fun, exploration and games amongst the whitewashed buildings and the oleander bushes of the hotel courtyard. There were climbing frames and crazy golf, table-tennis and swimming pools but the greatest joy of all was the freedom of the warm blue sea and being able to swim totally on my own for the first time. Not even a toe on the bottom!

At home again, another new adventure awaited me. My junior school was only a short walk away from our house and brought a mixture of fear and fun, joy and sorrow. The lessons were a challenge which I mostly enjoyed, but with the bigger boys and their rough playground games I was less happy. My teachers said I was a silent, shy mouse in contrast to my lively, bouncing ways at home. However, for the most part junior school jogged along quite happily until one terrible, fateful day.

There was a little boy at school of whom I was very fond. We would sit next to each other in class and always be partners; he was the only boy that I really liked. I arrived at school that day to be told by the teacher that he was dead. My heart sank, the classroom felt so empty – a horrible uncanny feeling. I went home and told my mother. There it was in the paper. A father had committed suicide, killing two of his own children at the same time: one of them was my friend Nicholas.

One theory is that anorexia nervosa stems from a childhood trauma, a hurt deep down inside. If such a theory were proved I am sure this event would have some significance. To discover death is a frightening and painful enough experience as it is, but when it is intertwined with suicide and murder, it becomes quite terrible.

It was around this time that I began to have bad

nightmares and fear the dark, as a lot of children do. Some
of the nightmares were so vivid that I can still remember
the smallest detail, like the colour of the carpet or the faces
of the people in the dream. One dream in particular
occurred several times over a period of a year or two. I
would be lying in bed, my father sitting beside me reading
a story. He would switch on the lamp next to my bed and
turn out the light by the door. When the story was over he
would say goodnight and switch my lamp off. Suddenly
the lamp would flash a ray of dazzling colours and a man
would step out of the wardrobe. He wore a black coat and
his eyes were dark and piercing.

"If I succeed I'll take you away; if I don't I'll be back
another day."

His voice was harsh and sly. He would place his hands
on to my stomach and press and press and press.

With anger and hatred he would say, "I'll come back
again and I'll get you next time."

Then he would disappear back into the wardrobe. I
would wake up with an excruciating pain in my stomach
and very scared. It is rather ironic that such a terrifying
dream – a repetitive dream – should be concerned with the
stomach!

My dreams nearly always expressed fear of the dark,
being murdered or desperately trying to escape from
something or someone. Another common dream that I
had around this time was being in the house, either alone
or with the rest of my family, when a burglar broke in. I
would always be the one to hear or notice him and would
creep downstairs to go and get help from the neighbours.
As soon as I had left the drive, he would be following me
but my legs would seize up and however much energy I put
into the running, my progress would be minuscule – I was
trapped. I always woke up just before being caught. The
situation would be very similar when the house caught fire
or if there was a murderer in the house.

In complete contrast, I also dreamt that I had abilities
no one else possessed, such as being able to fly. It was not

just a magical child's dream where I had instant wings and took off. I would nearly always be playing with my friends when suddenly an odd sensation would come over me – I would then bend my knees and put my hands on my hips, pushing my elbows out. A strange energy-force would enter my body, and I would keep pushing my elbows outwards. It took a lot of concentration and effort but gradually I would feel my feet leave the ground and I would rise higher. The odd thing was that I had to keep in the cramped position in order to be able to keep off the ground. I showed my friends what they had to do but they never seemed to manage it. I could not understand why they seemed so incapable of such an easy task.

I did not know anything about the psychology of dreams other than that dreams are supposed to reveal the subconscious feelings of a person. That was certainly proved when I was developing anorexia, as I dreamt quite often of the foods that consciously I just disliked or avoided. Subsconsciously, in my dreams, they were expressed with true hatred and fear. It seemed as though half the night was spent dreaming of potatoes that continued to accost me.

I do not know exactly what the nightmares and dreams at such an early age might have meant. I was obviously scared of being killed; perhaps I was afraid that I would be separated from my parents. I must have felt that someone was testing me, that what I did was no good, I was inferior to others, especially those of my own age. On the other hand, it would seem that I felt I did not belong in the same category as other children, expressed through the dream of being able to fly.

The dreams where I had powers that other children did not have or where I showed off or over-exaggerated, perhaps revealed that in reality I was trying to cover up my fears by putting on an image. I think this idea of covering up my feelings by putting on an image that was not really me carried on right up to and through adolescence, particularly when I was beginning to develop anorexia.

Despite my fears, I was a child really full of life and
buoyancy. I loved to let my imagination run wild and even
run away with me. I enjoyed making up games with one or
two friends, but most of all I adored to amuse myself. I
made stories up with my toys, I would spend hours sitting
in the car pretending to drive it and acting all the daily
events of an adult. Day after day I amused myself by
painting and drawing. Often I would write little notes or
stories and scribble a picture on the back. One read, "Dear
mummy, I like you and we have had a very happy
Christmas." I could not quite work out what the sketch on
the back was supposed to be though! Another read, "Dear
mummy, I love you because you love God."

Saying my prayers with my mother meant a great deal to
me and it brings back peaceful and happy memories. A
picture which my godmother had given me hung on the
wall beside my bed; I loved to look at it. It portrayed such
beauty and love. In it, Jesus is standing with the face of a
young child clasped between His hands and three other
children beside Him. His eyes are staring into the eyes of
the child between His hands. His look is warm and caring,
promising her life. So often I imagined myself to be this
child and I really felt that Jesus was taking care of me.

2

It's getting dark

It's getting dark
As the sun sinks low;
The moon doesn't shine
Nor do the stars glow.

My mind is a mirror
Of a saddened world;
My pain, a secret
Never to be told.

I am but a child
Whose heart is bleeding;
Affection is the food
That I need feeding.

During the last two years of my time at junior school Ruth had moved to boarding school. On the days when my school fellows teased me about my eyes, or when I felt self-conscious over reading in class because I was slower and more hesitant than most, I found myself longing to join her. I had visited the school on several occasions and wanted to be like the children there, with their smart uniform, brown shoes and straw boaters. I watched with envy the way they all entered the chapel on a Sunday with a partner in a long straight line. Clutching their hymn books in their hands, they bobbed as they passed the altar on the way to their seats. I longed to be an angelic-looking convent schoolgirl.

When my mother was able to take a full-time teaching job, my parents decided that it would be possible for me also to go away, so I sat the school entrance exam. To my delight I was accepted to start the following September.

As the time to begin the new school drew closer, my toes twitched with excitement. It was like the build-up to a grand finale. I finished my last project, took part in the school sports, received my Amateur Athletic Association Star Award and performed in my last little ballet show for which my friend's mother had made us both special tutus decorated with sequins. I was sorry to be leaving the ballet school for I loved to dance.

At last the big day came, my trunk was full, the clothing list checked off and we were on our way. Four hours later we turned into the school drive, passing the junior school, the hockey pitch on the left and the grass tennis courts on the right. We followed the car in front to the car park of the senior school with a trail of cars behind us. Children dressed in uniform were dodging between each car. It felt strange to think that I was now one of them.

Each form unpacked their trunks in a different room in the school; my trunk was deposited in the junior dining room. One of the sixth form showed me up to my dormitory. She led me up a long flight of stairs and turned right, passing a row of about eight washbasins. At the end of the corridor was a small, very steep, set of stairs, dark and dingy, leading to an attic, where there were two dormitories, commonly known as the "Archangels". On the right at the top of the stairs was a small bathroom, and straight ahead were the water tanks mumbling away to themselves.

I was in the second dormitory. I found the bed with my name on it, and dumped my suitcase on top. It was a strange room, with very low ceilings and sloping walls and the windows were tiny. At the end of each bed was a chest of drawers.

I said goodbye to my father, then set to work unpacking my trunk, placing my bedspread on the floor beside it and loading in my belongings. Each time it was full, I gathered the corners to the centre and dragged it up the stairs to the "Archangels". When the last few pieces had been taken up, one of the sixth form came over and ticked off each item on a list. It seemed a tedious and unnecessary job. At lunch it felt strange sitting amongst people of a mixture of ages, none of whom I knew. I was very shy and certainly had no gift for making conversation; I did not speak until I was spoken to. Then one of the sixth form asked me my name and age. I told her, explaining that I had been ten years old two days before. The only other piece of information I could offer was that I had an older sister in the school called Ruth.

After lunch I met the matron, who welcomed me: "It's nice to see you with us at last Helena." I felt quite proud to be one of the new girls and that Matron had noticed me.

Our classroom was at the far end of the school block, commonly known as the Barratt block. It was opposite the music practice-rooms and next to the cookery room. I found a desk near the front and put my pencil-case, ink and some paper inside it. There were very few desks in the room, as there were only about twelve girls in the class. It was a class in-between the junior school and the senior school, known as lower remove.

I settled in very quickly and at first did not feel at all homesick. I did not really feel out of place either, as I knew the building and some of the staff through visiting my sister. Ruth had also told me a lot about the routine of boarding school life, so I knew just what to expect.

The one thing that did take time to get used to were the lessons. Many of the subjects were new to me, and most of the other girls had either been to the junior school attached to this school or had covered some of the work before. I began to get rather left behind. My confidence diminished as my work was returned with large red crosses through it and endless circles round words which were incorrectly spelt. I had been taught the ETA method of spelling at my previous school which concentrated on the sound rather than the spelling of words. I remember during my first term at boarding school, the headmistress set us an essay "A nonsense story". The comment at the end of my essay read, "Some good nonsense here, Helena, but some of your spelling is nonsensical too! Try very hard to improve it." I was forever being told that my ideas and imagination were good, but my grammar extremely poor.

It was not long before several of the girls in the class started to tease me. I don't know whether this was because I was the youngest in the school, because I had an older sister, or because I was the ideal person to pick, being very quiet and too scared to tell anyone I was being bullied. To begin with, they just teased me over my work and hid my uniform so I was late for lessons and was told off by the teachers.

Later in that first year two other girls arrived who were equally shy and gullible and they also became targets for bullying, although I remained the chief one. In the

morning, either my school shirt or shoes were hidden. I
would search all over the dormitory for them with no
result. The only thing I could do was to put on another
shirt, either next week's school shirt (which was a different
colour), or games clothes. Whatever I wore, Matron
always noticed and sent me back upstairs, saying I could
have no breakfast unless I was dressed properly, so I often
had to miss breakfast. The girls frequently messed up my
school work with ink blots, so I was criticised for untidy
work. If I cried it made the situation worse for it showed I
was weak and a good target, so I learnt to hide my feelings
and only to cry at night. Matron would often ask me if I
had been crying but I did not have the courage to say yes or
tell her the reason why.

The situation gradually became worse. In the morning
I would be shut out of the dormitory along with the two
other girls while we were down on the landing, washing.
The others refused to let us in until the lining-up bell for
breakfast had gone, which meant we had to make our
beds, dress, and get to the refectory, all in five minutes.
Consequently we were often late, and either told off or not
allowed into breakfast, depending on how late we were.
At night the girls told ghost stories to frighten me, and
made apple-pie beds. When it was lights out I would leap
into bed and either put my foot through the sheet or have
to curl up and pretend to be in bed, remaking it after
Matron had switched out the lights. One girl in particular
used to take my bedspread and hide it, and throw powder
puffs at me or put soggy tissues under my sheets. I began to
dread the night as much as I did the day.

Looking back, I think the torment and emotional
difficulty that came with my first year had quite a lot to do
with my developing anorexia nervosa, in as much as it
damaged my self-confidence. Whether anorexia is basic-
ally physical or not, I still think that events such as these
are contributory factors as they lead to unhealthy self-
criticism, a feeling of worthlessness, emotional problems
and depression. Eventually these climax in stress. As a

friend once said, "Stress is like the pressure building up in a bottle, and unless it is let out gradually then the pressure becomes so great that it cannot remain inside the bottle any longer, resulting in the cork shooting off and the contents flying out: it explodes." The results do not show immediately; the build-up is gradual but has a drastic effect.

I began to feel that there must be something wrong with me for the other girls to dislike me so much. I began to blame myself, concluding that I was a useless piece of material that had been rejected by all. Yet I was unable to convey my feelings to anyone and so relieve some of the pressure. Instead I learnt to hide my feelings, a disastrous thing to do.

Ruth had already told me that bullying was bound to happen and that it had happened to her. I felt it was no use my trying to talk her into helping me. Besides, if I went and cried on her shoulder I would be showing my inability to defend myself. I wrote to tell my parents that I was unhappy and hated my class, but Ruth said I could not send it to them as it would hurt their feelings too much. They had decided to send me away to school and were paying a lot of money for my education, and the girls in my class were bound to leave me alone sooner or later.

So I decided there was nothing I could do about the bullying other than push it aside and enjoy all the other aspects of school life. Popularity isn't everything, I told myself. I was chosen as goal-shooter for the netball team, which really pleased me; I found my piano lessons exciting; I enjoyed the touch tapestry that I was doing as a hobby, and I began to get some good marks in lessons. My morale was very much boosted when I received a commendation for a short essay.

As I was rather young for the class, and to consolidate my learning, I stayed down in the lower remove for another year along with the two girls who had arrived a term late. It might have seemed a shame to stay down but at the same time it was a great relief to see the back of most of my class. I was no longer the youngest and I knew exactly what to expect as far as school routine and lessons were concerned. I could play a dominant role, showing the new girls what to do. I no longer felt pushed around, but in command, and I made some good friends.

We had a new form teacher whom I liked very much. As I had done most of the work in the previous year, my marks began to improve but the teacher also gave me confidence because she encouraged my love of art and acting. She seemed to have confidence in my work which boosted my morale.

Amongst my class friends I was happy, although still very timid. However, I found myself living more and more in an imaginary world. It was partly my love of acting and partly my need to aspire to a different world from that in which I was living, where I could be the person that I wanted to be rather than the person I was forced to be. I used to make up stories and act them out with one or two friends. We often went out on to the hockey pitch where we had space to imagine that we were on "the vast prairie" as the characters in a current television series.

As I was continually pretending to be someone else my parents' idea that I might like to attend a drama summer school greatly appealed to me. This was an exciting new adventure. Out on the huge lawns in the blazing sun of that summer we learnt many aspects of the theatre. Fencing and judo were new techniques which we developed alongside the more familiar acting and dancing. There were two real highlights of the course, the coming together of the different age groups for the filming of *Julius Caesar* and the end-of-course stage production. In this I was chosen to take the lead, a fantastic experience, especially in the setting of that stately building in the beautiful Worcestershire country-side. As a result of this holiday I decided to take speech and drama as an optional extra at school.

These lessons became a delight to me as the bewildering new school year got underway. Larger classes, new subjècts and a form mistress I was frightened of – along with the rest of the class – shook my earlier confidence.

Amongst my many other sports, I joined the gymnastics club, and began taking part in the BAGA awards. School life was very busy, despite the difficulties, and when annual events came round, I enjoyed them enormously. One such event, and perhaps my favourite, was harvest festival. It was lovely to think that autumn had come, that the harvest was over and most of all that food could be collected and given to those in need. I loved to help decorate the chapel at the convent ready for the service on Sunday morning. The headmistress would ask for volunteers to help, and we would load up wheelbarrows at the school with fruit and flowers that had generously been given. The window-ledges and sisters' choir stalls in the chapel would be decorated in the most artistic fashion possible. As one entered through the door at the side, a fresh, fruity smell would waft past. The combination of fruit and straw really made harvest come alive.

Gradually, I began to come to terms with the large classes and various changes. Although nervous and self-conscious, I began to find my feet.

3

I don't think anyone will know

I don't think anyone will know
Why the hurricane does blow
And the child's heart is cold as snow.
I know she has tears in her eyes
And her mind's filled with despise,
For happiness seems never to arise.

She cries herself to sleep at night
And in her dreams continues to fight.
The battle's long and will not end,
Fate appears to be round every bend,
The path gets yet harder to climb,
"Please God save her in time."

The transformation from child to teenager produced dramatic changes in feelings and attitude to life, changes which took place over a period of several months, not simply at the appearance of my first menstruation.

In the August of my thirteenth year to my great delight we had our annual holiday in Majorca. This was our second holiday abroad and embarked upon by us all with eager anticipation. The location lived up to our expectations. The hotel was at the end of a beautiful deep inlet of crystal-clear blue water. Too soon, however, I was aware of an agonising pain in my abdomen and although the lunch menu was tempting I had no appetite. When we went upstairs to unpack I realised that I had started my periods. I was dumbfounded, although I knew all about puberty and was not disgusted. However, before menstruation actually began I had given little thought to the subject, and the gap between childhood and adulthood had seemed very large, the changes far into the future. I could not imagine these things happening to me, or my body being that of a mature woman.

I told my mother and she put me at my ease instantly, so I was pleased to be venturing into womanhood and embarking on a new phase of life. The sea and sun relaxed me and as a family we had great fun swimming far out to boats moored in the bay, searching the clear waters with goggles and snorkel for coral and spiky sea-urchins, going for walks along the rocky headlands where we could pick wild figs and almonds. We were united as one happy family.

Back in the usual humdrum world of school, the changes in my body and mind became more evident. Although relieved that I was normal, I feared growing up because I felt that I was not ready to face the pressures adulthood would bring. I was happy to be a child and had no reason to change or lose my simple yet exciting way of life. Growing up threatened my security.

Many of the lectures at school on puberty and sex had been interesting and yet also threatening because I feared that such things would be forced on me before I was ready to cope. I was too wrapped up in activities such as sport, dancing and drama to take any real interest in boys and had no desire to be sexually attractive; at times the thought almost disgusted me.

I was always very conscious of my shape and appearance and extremely sensitive to other people's comments about either clothing or slimness. I was content with the shape of my body which was slim and not very well developed. I had no desire to increase in weight but neither did I have any reason to weigh myself, therefore I rarely stood on the bathroom scales.

My classmates frequently attempted to slim and in order to join in I occasionally announced, "I am going on a diet tomorrow," with little intention of carrying it out. It was more an adolescent reaction to having overeaten that day, and never lasted more than a couple of days because I knew there was no need to restrict myself. It is true that I later became self-conscious of my waist and thighs and occasionally grumbled about my inherited large rib cage but made no real effort to become thinner.

But teenagers are under tremendous pressure from both the media and their peers to keep their bodies slim. Every magazine I opened at that time was urging me to lose a few inches from my waist and thighs, telling me that life would be more wonderful and that I would be more desirable if I had the ideal figure. Some people in my class said that I had the best figure in the group whilst others were highly critical. The pressures of the group, at times, would override my own knowledge that my healthy appetite and physical activity balanced one another well. Confusion and indecision reigned in my mind.

The new-found feelings which arose at this time brought with them fear, confusion and depression, resulting in bizarre eating habits, periods of lack of appetite, as well as a tremendous need to be noticed and loved. It was as if something clicked out of place at times; almost as if there was a fault in the body mechanism which led to the secretion of some substance producing obscure feelings which were in themselves a warning sign that anorexia nervosa was underway.

There were times when I felt an agonising sense of loss, like a child might experience whose whole family had died suddenly in a car accident. An inner pain would sweep through my whole being in an intense longing to love and be loved, despite the knowledge that my family dearly loved me. Perhaps it was this, combined with an inability to communicate my innermost thoughts with friends, that made me frequently wish I was someone else. I felt hollow, lonely, lost; an emptiness surrounded me which needed to be filled. It seemed as though others were complete and I had no point of contact; I was the lost and lonely soul on the outside. The feelings would change dramatically and for no apparent reason to a mood of happiness in which I was bouncy and self-confident. Then just as suddenly I would become sad again, shut in a world of my own.

These feelings led to a deep sense of insecurity and inferiority which in turn led to extreme sensitivity. I felt that I was worthless compared with others in my form and my sister who was taking so many O-level subjects which seemed out of reach to me.

As my feelings of inferiority grew so my inability to communicate with others increased and I found myself needing to be noticed, not just as a member of the lower fourth, one of twenty-eight thirteen-year-olds, but as an individual with my own needs and aspirations. I even found myself being sent out of lessons for not con- centrating or for being disobedient, which was not in my nature in the least but was obviously a good way of attracting attention. I half dreaded, half longed for the moment when I had to see the teacher at the end of the lesson, to come face to face with her as a person. The ridiculous thing was that normally I was such an obedient child, scared to do anything wrong. The "click" had produced a new being who would do even this to be noticed as an individual, and yet all my life I had been loved and at home my individual needs were catered for.

As the academic year progressed I had fewer and fewer reasons to be unhappy, yet my unhappiness increased. I was doing well in lessons, improving my grades continuously. I was walking away with five-star pent-athlete awards, I had passed the top BAGA award for gymnastics, and my speech and drama grade two examination with merit – yet endlessly I sought attention as though I was trying to say, "I might have achieved these things but what am I like as a person? Who am I? Please look at me and tell me what the real me is like."

4

In silence

I sit in silence
Wondering where
My love should lie;
Or does it
Sit in silence
And quietly die?

I sit in silence
And think of
Stolen years
My eyes
A gentle stream
Of dew-drop tears.

I sit in silence
A changing world
Before me blowing!
In my heart
Love and pain
Together flowing.

I sit in silence
Alone and staring
At an empty sky;
Confused, lost
I ask myself
Who am I?

The search for my own identity and difficulties over relationships were the two main features of the next year and I believe they both played an important part in my developing anorexia.

The problems encountered in relationships extended from home to school and were doubtless intertwined. The fact that my sister and I were so often at war made for a deep unhappiness which affected my ability to relate to other young people.

At this time I felt that Ruth regarded me with disdain. It seemed that nothing I did or said was acceptable and I began to feel that I was simply some brainless insect, good for nothing. The more I longed for her approbation the less I was likely to receive it. It seemed I was a nuisance, and almost always unwelcome. When in her presence, especially at school, I felt intense pain and anguish. Perhaps we should not have been at the same school, making life difficult for one another. The whole idea had been to bring us together after our earlier years of jealousy and fighting, but it seemed to be having quite the opposite effect. One of the sources of our clashes was probably her mistaken idea that I was favoured at home, a natural assumption for with all my hospitalisation and inability to sleep I had needed my parents', and in particular my mother's, attention more than most children. Perhaps my mother should have left me to scream or drawn Ruth into the situation more, or perhaps my father should have taken Ruth off and played with her more often to give her the feeling that she was equally important, but we know that people can only do what their strength and time permit and it is easy to have wisdom after the event. Whatever the answers, her child-understanding could only see a pampered little sister who seemed to receive more love; a deep hurt and bitterness developed which led to great unhappiness for both of us.

The relationship with my parents at this time was, in comparison with many other teenagers, reasonably good. However, it was not completely without its difficulties. These were not particularly obvious to the outsider nor even to my parents. I knew they loved me and I loved them but I felt that there lay a barrier between us. This barrier was probably due to many things. Being a long way from them in miles, I felt a long way from them as far as communication and personal contact was concerned. By not seeing them for quite long periods I no longer felt a part of them as I had done before, and therefore did not feel able to express my inner feelings to them. I felt far away from them as though I was on the end of a string but the string had knots in it and I was unable to pass those knots; they kept me away. I needed the security I found in them yet the need for independence overrode this much of the time, especially at school. In many ways I had to feel separate in order to discover who I was in the search for myself and needed to break off, find independence or put my trust in someone else.

Because of the feeling Ruth had that I was the favourite, I rebelled, in a sense, by a determination to prove that I wasn't. I hated myself for Ruth's misunderstanding and for being, apparently, the cause of her unhappiness. Therefore, I suppose in many ways I tried to avoid forming a deep relationship with my parents for it would mean a worse relationship with Ruth, for whose love I so much longed. Being in the middle of puberty, I tended also to reject in particular my father's love for me and shunned any sign of affection.

The saying, "sticks and stones may break my bones, but words will never harm me," did not apply to me in any way; it was the words and consequent emotional pain that left a scar.

That year I had a very deep scar left as a result of

relationships. I had just made good friends with one of the girls in my class, Michele. Although completely opposite in personality, we shared many of the same interests and understood each other well. Unfortunately, in becoming friends with me she broke off her friendship with another girl. This girl had never liked me and was determined that the last thing I was going to do was to remain friends with Michele. She made it clear that I was the one who had destroyed their friendship and that I was now hated. Whenever I walked into the room I had a horrible sensation that my presence was very unwelcome, and I was usually greeted with a scornful or sarcastic remark. In her eyes everything that I did was no good, my work was useless, my appearance untidy, my figure far from perfect and my clothes did not suit me. I was generally down-graded the whole time. The strange thing was that just before she left, two years later, she turned to me for help and reassurance, and we developed quite a good rela-tionship.

On one occasion I had been hurt by the same girl's remarks and I refused to go into the biology lesson. Then I came to my senses and told myself that my work was not going to suffer because of someone else's unkindness, so I walked in, a little tear-stained, but I could not concentrate on my work and instead wrote a poem.

The teacher was fully aware that I had not been concentrating on the lesson, and that this was not the first time; in fact, she had already spoken to me on more than one occasion about not concentrating on my work because of being upset. She did not shout at me, merely asked to see me after the lesson had ended. When everyone else had left and I was standing alone in the laboratory a sudden fear came across me and the words that I so wanted to say were tied round my tongue and refused to break my lips.

"Are you all right?" she asked.

"Yes," I replied.

"You're not unhappy are you?"

"No."

I heard the word "no" resound in the empty room and there was a deathly silence.

"You're shaking," she commented.

I wanted to tell her exactly what was going on, my difficulties and my new-found feelings, but she was a teacher and I felt that there lay a barrier between us. This was a bad impression to receive because teachers are concerned with the whole welfare of their pupils and I think it is very important that pupils feel able to discuss their problems. Being bashful did not help; I could not bring myself to say anything to her.

I wrote a lot of my feelings down on paper and found they were closely related to what people thought of me, in particular teachers, especially if they showed any sign of caring or concern for me. At the end of the year I burnt all my notes, in the fear that they might be read, especially after being teased by one of the girls in my dormitory over being one of the teachers' pets. The same teacher often used to talk to me after class.

I remember on one occasion there had been tremendous rivalry over friendships, and the situation had got out of hand. As usual I was the centre of the problem, and one of the girls had been extremely spiteful to me. I arrived late for the lesson feeling as if the world hated me, sat by myself and forced the tears back. I could not see the blackboard so did not write any notes. When I received my preparation back, it read "2/10 – rubbish". On top of everything, I was experiencing my first bout of real depression. By the time it came to the practical of the biology lesson, I couldn't take any more and walked out of the lesson into the cloakroom. I had worked myself up into such a state that I was physically sick.

The teacher fetched me and spoke to me privately after the lesson. I managed to explain the situation over friendships, my depressions and worry over work and exams. She soon put me at ease and said that if need be she could sort out the trouble that I was receiving from the girl in my class. She was concerned about my work and noticed that when I was unhappy my marks dropped dramatically, and this in itself was why I received low marks. She reassured me that there was no reason whatsoever to worry over exams.

I remember her saying I worried about trivial things, and also that my failing was comparing myself with others.

On the surface I portrayed a totally different image to that of the insecure child within. Several people had commented on how mature I was for my age, not physically, intellectually or the way in which I acted, but in the form of self-expression and sensitivity. Rather than joining in with the fun and games of adolescence I would prefer to express my inner feelings and my thoughts on a subject through prose, poetry or artistic media.

As a result of adolescence and the problems over relationships I found myself desperately searching for my own identity.

I began to question the value of my own existence. In reality I knew who I was, that I was a living human being, yet I constantly asked myself, "Who am I?" I had to find out what I was really like as a person before I would be able to live life to the full. My search went on and on through the everyday happenings of life and in the quiet of the night as I tried to discover who I *really* was: what I was really like deep down inside when the mask was removed; what reason I had for living; to whom I belonged; who loved me and whom I loved.

"Why don't I fade?" I asked myself, "Or have I faded?"

"Can people see me as I really am?"

"Can I see myself as I really am?"

"How do I know what I should really be like?"

"My heart floats in the air, it belongs nowhere."

In the search for identity the creativity within me played an important role. Through acting and poetry, painting and dance, I found that I was able to begin to catch a glimpse of that being which was myself.

5

Darkness in my mind

Darkness in my mind,
An endless black hole
That extends to eternity;
Deep and daunting.

Numbness throughout my body,
Dead, all feeling postponed,
Too heavy to rise;
Limp and lifeless.

My world was drowning in waves of depression and I was sinking into a deep hole; the muddy earth began to cave in on me and my vision was clouded. The falling earth pressed upon me, hammering me deeper into this fearful dark hole. The waves lashed around me; I was drowning, drowning in my own emotions.

Another disastrous lesson had just finished. I felt a tear trickle down my cheek, and bit my lip, forcing back all evidence that I was upset.

As I was packing up my books and leaving the room at the end of the lesson, the teacher called me to her.

"What's wrong Helena?" she asked.

"Nothing."

"It's no good saying that. Come on, I want to help you and listen sympathetically."

I told her that generally everything was getting me down. The dinner bell went in mid-conversation and she suggested that we made a move towards the refectory.

"I don't want any," I said.

"Don't be silly," she replied in a quiet but firm voice.

"I don't want any."

"Come on now, Helena, try just a little, just the pudding."

She took hold of my arm gently and I went to the refectory with her. Grace had been said and everyone was seated. A profound fear flowed through me and the smell of the food made me feel sick.

"I can't, I can't," I protested.

"Come on, I'll find somewhere for you to sit."

"No, no. Please, I don't want any."

The thought of sitting down and eating was enough to terrify me, but in the end she sat me at a table. I ate very little and felt very sick.

That afternoon the situation came to a climax. In the history lesson we had been given permission to do private reading. Nothing was said against doing school work as an alternative so I decided to finish my English prep. Suddenly the silence was broken by a harsh voice.

"What do you think you are doing, Helena?"

"My English prep," I replied in a very subdued voice.

"You deceitful child."

"Sorry," I said very apologetically. "I didn't hear y . . ."

"Are you deaf as well as all your other disabilities?"

My eyes filled with tears and I felt a great pain come over me with the teacher's last remark. There I was struggling to overcome my difficulties and be like any normal child and she gave the impression that I actually enjoyed having something wrong with me. The bell rang for the end of lessons and tears surged forward. I dried my eyes and one of my friends, Frances, came over and asked if I would like a game of tennis. I said that I would rather just sit for a few minutes but if she went and booked the court then I would love to play in half an hour.

However, the history teacher turned to me and said in a harsh voice, "You can get out of here now." That was the end. I left my books, got up and ran down the stairs, out of the building and on to the hockey pitch. I sat down by an old log and cried and cried. Frances came over to me a short while later.

"I hate it here, I really, really hate it," I said, the tears streaming down my face.

In the background I could hear music from the senior common room; the song being played was, "All by myself". The words sank painfully into me as the singer spoke of not wanting to be all by himself any more; not wanting to live feeling insecure. It was like a thorn passing into my heart.

My only means of coping with these feelings was through prayer and I started to go to the early morning chapel service twice a week. I believed in God but my belief had no real meaning and my prayers no depth; I simply knew that I had an inner need and found myself drawn to that place of peace and serenity. Somehow it gave me the inner strength that I needed to cope with life. During the silent moments I thought a lot about my paternal grandparents whom I had never known. Grandpa had died before I was born and Grandma never lived to see my third birthday. It saddened me that I had not known them whilst they were alive, yet I felt a strange closeness to them, especially Grandma, as though she was with me in all I did and understood my feelings. I knew them as people far better in a spiritual sense than I could have known them in an earthly one. I loved them and they loved me, and I knew they were with me through both the good and the bad times. The way in which I knew them as people was strange and there is certainly no way in which I can describe it, but the fact that I felt their presence, in particular Grandma's, when I was upset was fantastic.

I hardly knew my father's side of the family; all I knew was that I felt a part of them. I felt the same closeness and family link to one of my cousins, Kathie, as I felt towards Grandma and Grandpa. Late one night I sat on the edge of my bed feeling desperately unhappy and wrote and told her. I had rarely spoken to anyone of being depressed before because it was a new-found feeling that scared me and that I didn't know how to describe. I thought that, to an outsider, being depressed for no apparent reason must seem ridiculous and it must all be in my mind. Kathie told me in reply that it is normal to get depressed but the problem is trying to find the strength to overcome it, and we all need other people to help us. She described how our teenage years are the worst ones to get through because so many changes are happening to us, physical, mental and psychological. It is a time when we are questioning every aspect of life, because we are trying to mould our values for the future. She ended by saying it is how we learn to cope with our problems that is important.

The new realisation that I was going through a natural

process made it easier to cope with my problems and new-found feelings.

I hoped, having gained the knowledge that these feelings were part of life's experience and a step to maturity, that their intensity might lessen but this was not to be so. Although the new school year brought changes – our O-level subjects chosen, new teachers and new girls, dormitories over the other side of the school and freedom to walk to the local village in groups, my fifteenth birthday and two Duke of Edinburgh Silver Award Camps – I fell quickly from these heights into my dark hole.

During the two days of walking and camping for the Duke of Edinburgh Award I found I could not eat and lived off apples and dried milk, not even bothering to hydrate it. I had landed in "the hole" with a mighty thud. I stumbled in the darkness, falling over my own feet. The hole extended into a tunnel; either side of me and above was a wall as dense as one could imagine. At the far end was a small opening through which light was escaping, but it was too far in the distance to crawl to, let alone stretch out my hand and feel. I tried to ease myself back to where I had fallen in; I stretched my hand back to feel for the entrance, the empty space extended to eternity and when I turned my head there was not even a glimmer of light to be seen.

People, people overwhelmed! Wherever they might be, in any situation, as the feelings of inferiority filled me and I felt degraded and useless so people swamped me. Yet at times I would walk on air, held in the heights of joy, only to descend dramatically to the lowest depths. There was no intermediate stage, no middle road, no slow descent.

The pain in my mind would rip through my whole body, not pain as in a cut finger but an inner torture which yet was physical. Tearful and lost, my inner soul in torment, my whole being seemed to shriek for peace and stillness, contentment and serenity.

I needed to talk to someone and I longed to be with Kathie, but thousands of miles of sea were between us, and although she had told me to ring her whenever I needed to there were too many problems over doing so. Out of desperation I gave a note to the cookery teacher. Doing this was totally out of character: I did not like to show my feelings and was far too bashful to explain how I felt, but I think this was a real cry for help. I scribbled, in haste, on a piece of paper,

> Please help me.
> I can't stand another minute.
> Please don't tell anyone but the pressure of depression makes me feel sick and unhappy, and I hate the sight of food.
> I can't stand any more; I thought you would understand how I feel but if you think I am stupid just tear this piece of paper up and say nothing.

As I approached her with the piece of paper I thought I must be mad. She had already told me off once that day for not eating and said that she did not want me to fade away. As she pulled her bike out from under the shelter, I handed her the piece of paper.

"What's this? It's not my birthday," she said jokingly, and started to open it.

"Please don't open it until you get home." I said goodbye, and dashed inside. At least the situation was off my chest if nothing else.

The next day I received a letter from my other cousin, Sue, whom I had not seen for seven years and even then only briefly at her wedding. It was lovely to hear all her news. And that afternoon my restless mind was put at ease when the cookery teacher came up to me and said, "You come and see me some time."

After lunch I went along to see her. She was busy showing someone her wedding photos and afterwards she showed them to me. She pulled a chair towards her desk and told me to sit down.

"What's it all about then?" she asked.

"I don't know," I said, stuck for words.

She understood, and told me that we don't always know what exactly it is that is upsetting us.

"I think you worry too easily," she added, and asked what I was worried about.

"Work, I guess," I said.

"There are far more things than work, Helena. What else?"

I told her what had been on my mind recently. Then she asked about my parents and sister and went on to talk about tension and depression. She said that I was in a deep hole and needed to climb out, but was unable to do this alone.

At that moment the class bell went, but she said I would have to miss the next lesson and she would explain to the teacher where I had been. We went on to talk about jealousy and friendships and she advised me what to do.

"Sit at the front, smile and try to be happy, Helena."

I sighed.

"Do you know what I expect of my pupils, of you, Helena? To work hard? That's not the most important thing. Enjoy yourself, be happy!"

Just before I left I told her about not being able to eat.

"Of course you can't eat," she said, "because your stomach is all churned up, but try to eat a little."

I went through quite a long spell of not wanting to eat and avoiding meals. Food seemed both a friend and an enemy: sometimes it comforted me and at other times it accosted me. If for any reason I was upset or under pressure I tended not to eat, partly because I was not hungry and partly because the control over my appetite made me feel I was in command, which boosted my morale. At times I really hated the sight of food; it sickened me. On other occasions I had hunger pains but no appetite; my stomach craved food but my mind was not interested.

On one occasion I sat down at the dinner table and asked if I could have a small helping – I just toyed with it and when the sweet arrived I refused it. Someone on the table commented about my aversion to food and said that she thought I had got anorexia or "AN" as she called it. I knew very little about anorexia and adamantly denied the suggestion. However, I was reported to Matron for not eating and as a result had to sit next to her at mealtimes for several weeks.

It was around this time that I had more eating problems when staying with a schoolfriend. I enjoyed the easy-going lifestyle of the family but the thing which marred my stay was the fact that they tended to eat rather large meals composed mainly of "fillers" and I found this increasingly difficult to cope with. I felt guilty over the amount of food that I was consuming and often suffered from a bloated feeling and bad indigestion. Several months previously I had found that foods high in fat both nauseated me and gave me indigestion, so I decided, where possible, to cut them out of my diet. Obviously, over the months, my body had been accustomed to a fat-free diet and being laden with foods that it was not used to produced a negative reaction. I felt guilty over the amount of food I was consuming, not because I was on a strict diet with the intention of losing a set amount of weight, although I was concerned with not passing eight stone, but because I considered that I was losing my self-control. I felt that if I lost my control over a trivial matter such as eating, then I would lose my control over myself and I would, therefore, no longer *be* myself. I was constantly threatened: as soon as my self-control slackened I sensed a take-over bid from the impinging world. I was no longer who I was; my "self" had been snatched up.

Some girls had noticed my erratic eating patterns. One day the cookery teacher stopped me in the corridor.

"People have told me about you not eating," she said in a concerned voice.

I looked down and thought back to having to sit on Matron's table.

"Is not being able to eat upsetting you a bit?"

"Yes."

"Unless you start to eat there will be a lot of letters, and you wouldn't like that would you?"

"No."

The tone of voice suddenly changed.

"I loved your poem, Helena. You should take it up professionally."

"Thanks," I said, quite taken aback.

"Do you want it back?" she asked.

"No, you can keep it."

I thought that my unhappiness and depression would have eased a little, having been able to talk to someone, but I was mistaken: each day became more clouded, my anxiety increased, I became frustrated and at times resentful. To make things worse I developed a rash on my chest and eczema on my arms and back. At night I lay awake, tossing and turning, unable to sleep. Worse still, there happened to be scabies going round the school and I was unfortunate enough to catch it. I was staying with my grandparents when it started to develop and my grandmother was absolutely marvellous. She took me along to the doctor, painted the liquid remedy on and generally took great care of me.

It was lovely to see the Christmas holidays arrive. It had been a long dark term and I was looking forward to going home again. I really enjoyed myself, but a terrible time lay ahead.

I returned to school with exams on my mind. I could not get down to revision, I could not concentrate, and I seemed too tired to work for a long period. It was more of a mental fatigue than a physical exhaustion, and I found myself breaking down very easily. I felt as though I was in battle with myself. It was a subconscious, continual battle, and as it progressed so the outer me, the visible me, became frustrated and miserably dejected. If only I could have recognised what the inner me was fighting over and why. My brain could not register exactly what was going on. It was a strange feeling which left me in a helpless, isolated, dark world. Others stood in the light, yet I was trapped in the dark. I stretched out my hand so often to pull myself through, but back I would be pushed, landing with a mighty thud, as though I was a worthless being. The whole world disappeared from me: I watched it shrink into the background, becoming smaller and smaller. The more I became pushed down, the more I lacked self-esteem; and the lower I was pushed, the greater the need to succeed and the desire for achievement became.

The following description is of a picture that I painted at the time.

Isolated from the outside world, I am living in it, breathing in it, but I am trapped. A transparent shell surrounds my body, barricading me from all its beauties; such beauties I see but cannot reach. I stretch foward but my hand collides with the membrane, I cannot feel what my eyes see, I hear the melodious sounds but they do not penetrate. On one side of me there is food; on the other, water. I long to take them, but I cannot.

The days alternated between good and bad, as seen in these two extracts from my diary. It shows how quickly my mind changed as there was only a day between these passages.

I woke up to see the world enthroned in white, no difference between sky and earth. A sheet of mist hung over the trees making the buildings silhouettes. The snow was crisp and glistened with crystal sparkles as the rays of the golden sun shone amongst the trees and enlightened the world. A beautiful sign of God's creation.

A rather worrying day in health hazards; whatever I ate I had indigestion. Sometimes I feel like I am inside a shell and the atmosphere outside my shell is nasty and clings around. At other times I feel as though I am in a shell and the atmosphere outside is lovely, fresh, and peaceful; I want to break out but I am trapped.

As my confusion and unhappiness deepened, the more my sense of insecurity grew. I did not know where to turn and I felt a great loss. It was at these moments that I sat and thought about my cousin, Kathie. I thought of the stories that she told me in her letters about going to stay with Grandma and Grandpa every summer.

It was like going back in time a century, with all the photos of our ancestors on the wall in the hallway, the summer-house in the garden and the orchard in which Grandpa gave us our own apple tree. I can still picture him carving the Sunday joint, sitting in his armchair at the table, and going to the shops with me and Rusty, the dog, who could do just about anything. It is a pity that you didn't know Grandpa; he was a wonderful man.

As I read what Kathie had written to me it all felt so alive, and I felt so much a part of the family. It was as though I had been searching for something precious and at last I had found it. In many ways I had. I was searching for my own identity and I had found the roots of it, for although I am my own self, my traits lay here, in people I did not know.

It was not that I did not love my parents, but that I had been deprived of knowing that side of my family, and there was no denying that I was very much a part of them. It hurts me very deeply to say this now, but at the time to think of my parents and my sister was painful. Although I had wanted to go to boarding school, I felt bitterly hurt because of being separated from my parents at such a vulnerable age. Likewise, Ruth's vindictive attitude towards me resulting from her jealousy over the attention I received as a young child, pressed a deep pain into my heart, so piercing it bled tears. I blamed myself for the way she treated me; I was the one who caused her emotional suffering. So many times I sat and wept, "If only I had not been born then no one would feel hurt."

I was not at all surprised to find out that I had done badly in most of my school exams as I had been unable to revise for any length of time. My results were not bad enough to be referred to the headmistress, but being disappointed by my comparatively low marks I decided to discuss them with her. She said that I had obviously worked hard, but I did not realise the big jump between upper fourth and lower fifth and that she did not doubt my ability to do well next time. Then she went on to say that I gave her the impression that I was lonely and told me that I was too thin.

Just as I was leaving the room, the biology teacher walked in and the headmistress asked her if I was supposed to have seen her to discuss my results.

"No," was the reply. "But I know she's thinking life isn't worth living right now."

The previous biology lesson, the teacher had told me that I was capable of the work and the only reason my exam results were worse than usual was because I was depressed. She was too right!

6

Fading dreams

Yesterday's dreams fade
Beneath the skies,
New found realities
Of today arise.

In the breeze
The memories blow;
Far, far from me
They go.

As a recompense to the less attractive aspects of life, I held in my hands certain precious gifts which I released at times when I needed to let my inhibitions fly away.

Writing, art, dance and drama have always helped to release my pent-up feelings. Since early childhood, writing has been my solace and means of expression: right from the time in infant school when we wrote our illustrated news books, through the stages of making up little stories and long newsy letters home with lively little sketches incorporated, to a very special writing relationship I had with Doris.

Doris is the mother of one of the old girls, Mary, who was in the sixth form when I first started boarding school. Although a great deal older than myself she was, and still is, a great friend. I came to know her when she and my grandparents both moved to the same town. We kept up a frequent correspondence, writing just about anything to each other, from school to politics and from war to fantasy. We shared the same interest in writing and a keen appreciation of life. Many times I wrote to her reflecting on my inner feelings. Most of the time I did not write because I felt I wanted to; rather I felt compelled to in order to release my suppressed thoughts, ideas and feelings. I was only too grateful to have someone who could respect my need to write and appreciate my letters. It was through being free to express myself and through what Doris said in her letters that I realised the importance of finding oneself. At one time when I had only a year left at school, during which I was free really to be myself as Ruth had left and thus I no longer lived in her shadow, Doris obviously had the same thoughts over the matter as I did. She said in a letter:

Actually I think it is a good thing that you are coming here on your own for half-term and I think that now Ruth has left school you may feel less tense. This is no reflection on Ruth or you, but I think it is not always the right thing for sisters or brothers to be at the same school as each is often living in the shadow of the other. I saw that with some of my children and in my own case.

We quite often discussed depression: what causes it and how to cope with it, how one can be depressed for no apparent reason, and the connection between depression and the need for identity.

I think some of us live more deeply than others. We can achieve greater heights of happiness and real joy – but at the other end of the scale we can reach depths unknown to other people. When I see something breathtakingly beautiful, I can *feel* its beauty and my heart leaps with joy. I savour these moments when I am experiencing something of real meaning. When I feel down I know it will pass and I try to turn to something that I know gives me joy. That is not easy and not always possible, but do remember the feeling will pass.
Thank you for writing – go on writing and writing. I do believe it is a way of finding oneself, and some people can put on paper what they cannot put into words; the spoken word is so nebulous and intangible.

The aspect of English which I enjoyed most at school was writing essays. These enabled me to use my imagination and I would often find myself writing essays for sheer enjoyment on deeper subjects. In my early boarding school days I wrote some short stories amongst which, naturally, was one about boarding school life and more unusually, a fantasy called "The Time Eater". But the writing which has always given me most pleasure, helped me to unwind and at times has almost seemed a compulsion, is poetry. Often I would illustrate what I wrote.

To stand alone in a light, airy room with its large windows overlooking the ever-changing shades of the leaves on the trees, paper in front of me and paintbrush or pencil in hand, became a source of tranquillity and inspiration, my relief from emotional anguish. Because this type of painting comes from deep within the heart and is an emotional rather than an intellectual exercise, there is freedom and release. The movement involved, being physical, is in itself calming. As the work progresses, understanding of the feelings which have inspired it develops. On looking at the finished article one begins to understand the depth and content of one's own feelings. If I have a blemish on my face, I feel it and wonder what it is; it is not obvious. But on looking in the mirror I can see clearly what it is. So with the painting: that which was only half apparent and hidden in the depths of my being would be there for me to see on the paper. I had a better understanding; I felt cleansed and the frustration gone. Paper, paint, and I had a unity.

When I received my O-level design paper with two weeks' preliminary studies to do, there were several questions which I could have chosen. After much thought I decided to design the scenery for a setting of a play which was trying to convey the idea of modern soullessness. I thought I must be mad to have chosen that question as no one else attempted it, but my art teacher was delighted that I had made that decision; she had very much liked the only other stage-set design I had done. From the moment I started to work on the design I derived great satisfaction from it, firstly working on the theme in sketch form for the preliminary studies, then explaining in writing how the idea evolved and sketching out where the scenery would be placed on the stage. Then the backcloth was designed and finally I did a painting of the view that the audience would have of the set. I think it is the piece of design work that I have most enjoyed as I felt so much a part of it and I could really feel the theme developing each day.

Through working on that design many of my tensions and inhibitions were relieved. This made my school work in general far easier.

Dance through the ages has been an important mode of expression, from primitive war dances to the most sophisticated and graceful of courtly dances, or delicate expressions of love in ballet. So, too, dance has been one of my greatest delights. In the rigid structure of ballet and tap dancing lessons there was a challenge and discipline which were both demanding and rewarding. I found exhilaration and enjoyment in the shows we did in some of the neighbouring small towns, and there was always an air of fun and joy on the occasions when we danced out in the open air at village and church fêtes.

However, the greatest emotional satisfaction and means of expressing the inner turmoil, sadness or happiness within my soul has always, and still does, come from merely moving to either music or the inner music of the heart in that type of dance known as Laban movement. At school I would often go off alone into the art room, or perhaps the gym, and, unobserved, dance with freedom. This type of dance, or movement to music, of which we had a little in my earlier days at school, allows for great freedom and self-expression. As I dance the air flows through me and lifts my spirit as well as relaxing my body.

Poetry has been a great love since childhood when my mother would sit on my bed and read poetry to me; then we would alternate, she reading one poem and I the next. Later, in my speech and drama lessons at school, I frequently chose poems with themes to which I could relate so that rather than just reciting them I could feel what the poet was really trying to convey and became a "part" of the poem. I mostly chose poems with deep meaning and expression so that I could express my inner thoughts through another poet's words. It is perhaps interesting that for my grade three examination my subconscious led me to choose the poem "Hunger" by

Laurence Binyon. My tutor said that I read the poem beautifully, with great meaning, and the examiner commented that I had tremendous force in the last line which spoke of "being" hunger. At the time I did not know the irony behind choosing this poem but now I am sure it must have been a cry for help. There were plenty of times when I said I was not hungry and was unable to eat, and yet my body craved food. It really experienced the agony of hunger the pain registered in my subconscious mind.

As my speech and drama lessons progressed acting began to replace poetry as a form of self-expression. Once again I chose parts to which I could relate and in which I could become emotionally involved so that I experienced the feelings of the character I played. This also enabled me to give rein to my own feelings. The soliloquies from plays which I acted, either in preparation for an examination or for one of several school drama evenings, gave me an inner satisfaction far greater than that achieved in taking part in a complete play. This was partly because I always chose the most intense or heart-rending speeches which ended on a climax. Two of my favourite pieces, which I performed on separate occasions, were a speech of Olga's from Anton Chekhov's play, *The Three Sisters*, and Joan's speech on being condemned, from Bernard Shaw's play, *Saint Joan*. To my immense delight my performance of Olga brought much praise, in particular from the headmistress and english teacher, but it was the part of Joan which gave me the deepest sense of fulfilment. As I sat in front of the audience, curtains parted, I was filled with great fear, something which did not usually happen (a few nerves maybe, but not fear). For a split second my mind was filled with a jumble of thoughts. I felt that I could not go ahead with the part; I would have to leave the stage. I felt as though I had been sitting there speechless for an eternity. Suddenly my fear burst into the intense words of Saint Joan. I leapt into a standing position; chains around my ankles – Joan, the prisoner!

Another wonderful experience on a different level was the occasion when my mother and I went to Italy for a few days to see the Holy Shroud. We booked in at a hotel in Milan and went directly by train to Turin, to the cathedral in which the Shroud was on exhibition. It was a wonderful experience, with the figure of Christ so clearly marked on the ancient cloth. As I walked along and gazed up at it the "Our Father" was being said in Latin, and it left me feeling tranquil, yet full of joy. The following day we went on Lake Como in a boat and up the mountains in a funicular railway. The view from the top across the lake was tremendous and the sense of freedom exhilarating. The last day we went to a service in Milan Cathedral, then wandered around the city square, returning to England in the evening.

I spent part of one holiday helping in an old people's home and during part of another a friend and I managed to get a job at a printers and designers. At school, in addition to things I have previously mentioned as being areas of great fulfilment, I was achieving well in gymnastics and on the sports field in track events and long jump, both in the school and county sports. The art teacher had asked for my help in designing scenery for a French play and I had done quite well in a national art competition, my work having been on exhibition in the Royal Albert Hall, London, followed by a tour of London libraries.

There seemed to be many activities to occupy my time and my mind also began to be taken up with career prospects. I had been to consult a career analyst in London in an attempt to help me decide on the right O-levels and future plans. The report on me included the following:

On the interest questionnaire Helena had well above average performance for the literary and artistic activities, contrasted with below average performance for the scientific and computational activities. The pattern shows she is most attracted to creative careers where she can communicate her ideas and feelings through writing or artistic media.

As we discussed at the consultation, Helena is working very hard at her school studies. I would, however, advise her to consider dropping one or two subjects so that she can concentrate closely on the remainder. This is particularly important.

Drawing together the results from the tests and the points that emerged at the consultation, I would conclude that Helena is best suited to opportunities where she can make use of her creative, artistic flair. It is important, however, that her artistic and practical skills are directed towards a definite goal, so that she can see the results of her work and knows what she has to achieve.

At present Helena does not feel motivated to taking A-levels and I agree that this is an appropriate decision.

She then went on to suggest that I apply for a foundation course in art followed .by a two or three year course specialising in the branch to which I was most suited. As an alternative she suggested I took a course in window display or nursery nursing.

There were so many positive aspects to my life and so many good happenings, in addition to the bad ones, in the time leading up to my O-levels that in some ways it is surprising that there should have been such a dark battle going on within my body. It was as if my inner being was under attack. I was being torn asunder.

7

Illusions of reality

I have seen the mirage
Freeze and crack
That once reflected
The ray of light,
Appearances that comprise reality.

Green hills have faded
Into the distance
Covered by sheets
Of drifted snow
Intertwined with the dull grey sky,

Trees are faint
And flicker in the darkness,
The wind is but
An eerie lull
And birds have no music in their hearts.

Words that I have
Long believed
Become engulfed
In the mist
And fade into invisible air.

The stream flows
Down to stillness
And dissolves
In the uncanny sea
Enlightened by the sinking sun.

Despite the fact that everything good seemed to be lying directly ahead of me, from the moment my O-level year started the world began to cave in. I was stranded on a barren island, but even that started to crack beneath my feet. I was totally confused as to why I felt such heartache and agonising emotional torment. I was at school alone, work was going well, even though I had not dropped two subjects as the career analyst had suggested, since I wanted to take them all. I was no longer in a dormitory but shared a study bedroom and I had the freedom of the nearest town at weekends, not that that was much compensation. An American acquaintance once said to me, "It's half the size of New York Cemetery and twice as dead!"

I felt an unbearable, aching loneliness. My inability to communicate with my class companions grew daily; I could not reach them, nor did I feel a part of their world. My confusion over life grew, and the waves of depression became ever more overwhelming.

A climax of unhappiness and depression had built up and in desperation I wrote a letter to the problem page of a teenage magazine. It was more to relieve the pressure than anything else. A short time later I received a reply.

Dear Helena,
Thanks for your letter. I think you should seek professional help because obviously you have a serious problem here. Go to your doctor as soon as possible and tell him all about your worries, just as you told them to me. Make sure you explain fully about the depressions and headaches, and ask him if he thinks he should refer you to a psychiatrist.
Now, I know that sounds pretty drastic and please don't

think I'm saying you're mad! I do, however, think that
psychiatric treatment could help you sort out a lot of
your troubles, and there's nothing at all to be afraid of.
I hope this helps you.

I was relieved when the letter came, but rather shocked
when the person suggested that I should see a doctor and
psychiatrist. Whilst I was writing to the magazine I did not
give a thought as to the reply; nonetheless I had not
expected quite such a dramatic answer. It put me in a very
difficult situation as there was no way that I could get to
see a doctor whilst at school unless I told Matron. That
meant explaining the problems to her which I could not
bring myself to do. On discussing the subject with one of
the young assistant matrons, she advised that I go to see a
doctor. She mentioned that she could arrange it, but
would have to speak to Matron and the headmistress first. I
said I would rather forget the idea. She went on to say
something that has always stuck in my mind.

"You know there's only one person who can really help
you – God."

I thought of what Kathie had told me in her letter as
well: "The only way you can find the strength to cope with
life is through faith and the overwhelming love of God."

So I decided to cope on my own and I asked God to give
me the strength to do so.

If I had wanted I could have gone to a doctor at home,
but the end of term seemed such a long way off and the
odds were that I might be fine by the time I actually got
there. Besides which, I did not want to say anything to my
parents about the problem as I remembered what Ruth
had told me that first year at boarding school, "You can't
tell them you're unhappy. It would hurt their feelings too
much."

From that moment I'd decided I could cope alone and I
had no intention of causing them any upset. I was also
aware that my problems were very much wrapped up in
family matters and my past. It was too painful to think

about it, let alone say anything.

During the holidays I was happy, apart from the times that Ruth and I argued, and I got on well with my parents; but I always felt a buried bitterness. Being at school away from my parents, and that year from Ruth as well, I had time to think about my bitterness. Why did I feel so distant from my parents even six years later? Why did my sister despise me so much, when all I had done was to be born? Why did I feel so desperately hurt?

Once I looked into the mirror and saw a dejected face. I felt great pain for no apparent reason – it totally mystified me. I stared and stared into the sorrowful, piercing eyes that seemed to outstare me. I looked down, then once more looked bashfully at this face in the distance, so divorced from me. I watched a tear trickle down the sallow cheek; my heart felt torn with agony – the eyes were red and glowing with dewdrop-like tears. I turned away and moved towards the door; quickly I glanced back at the mirror. To my horror, I realised that I was a part of that mystical picture by which I had been fascinated. But why was I crying? I was not upset. No, not upset but in agonising torment, and I had no control over these abstract and disturbing feelings.

I was working very hard for my early O-levels, revising every spare minute of my time. I preferred to work during the lunch break, eating some fruit, rather than go into the refectory for a meal. I found the small-talk at the dinner table monotonous and although I was hungry, I had no appetite for food. A plateful of meat and vegetables, the strong smell wafting past my nose, was more than I could tolerate.

Towards the end of lunch break, after school or at weekends, I quite often went over to the junior house to spend some time with the younger members of the school. I love children and it brought me great satisfaction to help them with their hobbies, teach them tunes on the recorder or play duets on the piano. The affection that some of them showed me made me feel appreciated. I often called into one of the classrooms after lessons to see a friend of my grandmother, Veronica, who also taught at the junior house. I liked sitting, talking to her and quite often she had a letter for me from my grandmother.

Through observing the simple, carefree lives of the younger children, I longed to be the same – to be able to accept myself as I was and live life to the full. It is not easy in today's affluent society. There is much emphasis on competition and success, especially in schools. It has been said that success boosts our ego, whilst failure lowers it. Those who fail have their self-confidence flattened because they are led to believe that if their work is useless, then they, as people, are useless; their hopes are defeated, destroyed.

My self-consciousness led me to believe that unless I was at the top of the class my work was useless. Even when I was at the top I still felt that my work was not good enough. Which meant that as a person, I was not good enough. I watched other people continually coming top of the class with little effort and certainly no gratitude; whilst I worked twice as hard with no worthwhile result.

So much emphasis is laid upon achievement that I feel the values in life easily get out of proportion. We are indoctrinated to believe that our lives depend on the height that we reach on the ladder of success. I think that the desire for achievement can override and even distort our personality. This is particularly significant in anorexia. Some doctors and psychiatrists believe that emphasis on success is one of the underlying causes of anorexia. I do not entirely agree with the statement; I would say that it puts one under considerable pressure and therefore increases the level of stress. It is said that anorexics are nearly always of above average intelligence with pressure on a high academic achievement from either home or school. Rather than seeing the anorexic rebelling against being the best, I see her striving for perfection, but never quite reaching either her own standards or those expected of her. This results in a lowering of her self-esteem, putting her under even greater pressure.

I lost all sense of being appreciated and loved as an individual. Yet rather than facing up to depression and trying to deal with it, I would turn my back on it and try to deny its existence, persuading myself that it had gone away.

I soon discovered that in working extra hard, virtually non-stop, I managed to hold my depression and unhappiness at bay. I woke very early in the morning and immediately started to exercise or do school work. I took a keen interest in every subject and directed all my mental energy into lessons, prep and revision. I spent the evenings dancing, reading, sketching or writing poetry. I did not really mind what I was doing, so long as my time was fully occupied and I could push my troubles to the bottom of the bottle. As the pressure in the bottle increased I wrote in my diary:

> You know every day I have been so tired, depressed and had headaches recently. I know in myself there is something infinitely wrong. Every day it gets worse and I don't understand why. Everyone gets depressed sometimes, and I did over short periods for about two years, but now it happens every day. I have so little energy and I can't take the pressure of absolutely anything any more. Why, Why, Why?

In the autumn of my O-level year I had taken three subjects to get them out of the way and during this time the standard of the remaining subjects tended to improve as I began to derive great satisfaction from aiming for high marks. The end of term seemed to arrive quickly, but likewise so did the end of the Christmas holidays. Although no one said anything at the time, my mother noticed that I had lost weight around the face and that I was eating a lot of meat and less carbohydrates. Ruth noticed that I had stopped eating sweets, desserts and cakes. Quite frequently in my diary I wrote of feeling bloated, sick or not being hungry. Towards the end of the holidays I received my three early O-level results: art, grade B; RE, grade B; and to my shame, english language, grade D. I was very disappointed with the results as I had hoped for at least one A and two Bs. It gave me the determination to work hard for my mocks and get no less than grade B in any of my remaining O-levels.

To my delight the Easter term began well. I had decided not to worry about the future, nor look back on the past; I would take each day as it came. I really enjoyed getting involved in my O-level work and began to take note of what I was writing rather than just taking down dictation and revising parrot fashion. Although I felt a lot better in myself and far more healthy than I had done for some time, at my first tap dancing lesson the teacher said she thought I had lost a lot of weight. A few days later one of the girls in my class commented that I looked ill. I did not know whether or not I had lost any weight, but I felt fine. I had taken quite an interest in food and a liking to cookery. I spent hours looking at recipes for a vegetarian cookery book that I was planning to put together for my mother, who a year or two previously had been put on a vegetarian diet for health reasons. I was becoming more and more of a health food addict.

I suddenly found that in spite of all the mental energy I was putting into my work, I had a vast amount of physical energy. This was a restlessness which became a compulsive need to exercise. A friend and I decided to do keep-fit exercises in the gym each day, gradually building up the amount each session and the number of sessions per day. To begin with I found that the more exercise I had, the more I was able to eat and the less I suffered from indigestion; this, however, was not maintained. Yet I began to feel that I was in control of myself for not only had I managed to organise an exercise routine but also my free time and school work. Despite my disappointment over my english language O-level result, I began to feel that there was still hope when the teacher told me that it was not my english that needed improvement and that in fact my compositions were very good. My morale was given a boost when I received the first chapter of my O-level history project back marked, "Excellent. Well written." Things were certainly looking up.

I went to stay with my grandparents for the long weekend break. Since they had some scales, I decided to weigh myself. Towards the end of the Christmas holidays I had noticed that I had lost a few pounds and was eight stone. This time I was seven stone, ten pounds. I was pleased that I had lost weight without even trying. When I returned to school I found that the tenor of life had changed. In my diary I wrote: "I had a bad night and woke up feeling ill. The thought of lessons really got me down and I felt weak all day. I had to do some revision, but I was so tired I lay down."

The same week we all had to be checked by the doctor for scabies as someone in the school had caught it again. This meant lining up with our shirts off. One of the girls in my class looked at me and said, "Cor! Helena, your ribs, you must be anorexic." The doctor did not notice that there was anything wrong with me so I thought no more of her statement. The mock O-levels began a few days later and all my energies were directed towards revision for them. I got up early in the morning to revise, usually around 6.00 a.m., at times as early as 5.00 a.m. I would slip my school uniform on and creep down the stairs, either alone or with a friend, and work in the library until the rising bell went when the silence would be shattered. Then after this I would jog round the hockey pitch to get some oxygen to my brain and keep myself fit.

At the end of the first day of mocks I had a tap dancing lesson and my teacher commented again that I had lost a lot of weight and said I had better not lose any more. A year or two previously she had noticed that I had an eating problem and had talked to me about it. I could not see what all the fuss was about as I did not feel as if I had lost any weight at all. However, I was aware that I was not eating much and quite often missed meals. The next day my speech and drama tutor commented on how thin I looked. Each day I worked non-stop, except for the odd meal, from 6.00 a.m. until 9.00 p.m. Then I would have a cup of herb tea and sit and talk for an hour before going to bed. Almost every night I would go to bed with a crashing headache and feeling freezing cold.

I used to pile layers of clothes on my blue limbs and curl up at the bottom of the bed, yet the cold gripped my body and ate deep into my flesh and bones. I would stuff my ears with cotton-wool to block out the noise from the corridors and other rooms and very rarely succeeded in getting a good night's sleep. I was always awake and ready to be on the move in the early hours of the morning. My whole sleeping pattern had been disrupted.

One thing that began to concern me a little was that I had not menstruated since Christmas and it was now the end of February. I did not really worry about it, but kept telling myself everything would be all right next month. At my next dancing lesson the teacher once more commented on my appearance, asking how much I weighed. As I did not have access to scales at school I truthfully told her that I did not know. Her reply was, "Weigh yourself before you die." That scared me, but the feeling soon wore off. I still could not tell that I had lost much weight despite my clothes having become looser; my perception of size was already distorted. If anything I felt better for having lost weight, not so much physically but mentally.

The day mocks ended, half-term began. No sooner had I walked into my grandparents' house than my grandmother remarked on how thin I looked and asked me whether I had lost weight. I weighed myself; I was seven stone five pounds. I felt very close to my grandparents that half-term and apart from doing a small amount of work I spent nearly all of the time with them. My grandfather had declined rapidly since I last saw him and I felt deeply for him. He was an extremely intelligent man, and to see the frustration over his loss of memory and his struggle to walk in contrast to his breathtaking stride of the past, was very sad. Despite this sadness it was an extremely memorable time for me. I wanted to help restore his confidence in himself. I played Scrabble with him, ignoring any mistakes that he made and constantly asking his advice to boost his morale. We took short walks in the sea air, his arm securely linked through mine. We sat and talked about various things; he showed me how to do artwork in copper and told me that I should write children's books. I helped my grandmother to prepare meals and sat and talked to her about writing and painting. I really felt that I had benefited a lot from that time with them. One problem was that because of eating fairly normal meals I suffered terrible stomach pains.

With my mock O-levels behind me, my main aim was to complete my history project and concentrate on my speech and drama grade five exam to be taken later that term, as well as working hard for my O-levels the next term. As a part of our history coursework we watched *Holocaust*. I found it really interesting but the brutal, bestial way in which the Jews were treated by the Nazis was agonising to watch and the scenes very much played on my mind. I began to shut myself off and I could not summon up any enthusiasm for a social life with my schoolfriends. I could not join in with their laughter, my spirits were too low and I did not find what they said funny. My depressed mood had returned and I could not snap out of it; instead my mind wandered off to dwell on hopelessness and despair. The world was determined to be against me, and I cried tears of confusion all alone. This time I was not going to deny my feelings; I had to face up to them and do something about their existence. So once again I decided to concentrate hard on my studies, filling my spare time painting or exercising.

I had started to pass out, especially during and after games lessons. I tried to keep this secret and where possible avoided hockey lessons by asking if I could play badminton instead with a friend. This was a lot easier, especially when we talked for some of the time, and sometimes I missed the lesson altogether. Once when I felt faint in the middle of the lesson, the teacher sent me to Matron who dosed me up with glucose. She told the teacher that I had been working too hard, but the teacher insisted that it was more than hard work and said that I had lost about two stone and looked very ill. I was so cold and dizzy that I could not bear to go into lunch that day; instead I got into bed to keep warm and ate an orange. Fruit was about the only food that I could tolerate without a feeling of revulsion or nausea, and I virtually lived on it.

I knew I had to keep going until the end of term, despite having begun to feel desperately ill. The vast amount of energy which I had had at the start of the term had vanished and my dancing was the only exercise that I could manage to keep up. I frequently felt drained, my head heavier than my body, and I was continuously cold, a coldness that sank deep inside me. My limbs were worst affected; they had a constant purple colouring. I could see that I looked tired and drawn but not that I was thin. When I looked in the mirror I saw plenty of flesh. I did not feel particularly thin and as far as eating went I kept my difficulties as well hidden as I could.

My form mistress stopped me in the corridor and asked if she could see me alone. I had dark rings under my eyes, my cheeks were sunken, my school uniform hung on me shapelessly. I felt terrible. She said that I looked very pale and thin, that I was like a shadow and advised me to be sure that I ate enough and did not work too hard.

After lessons, nine of our class were going on a retreat at the guest house, a part of the convent in the nearest city. Earlier I had received a phone call from my boyfriend saying that he was coming up to see me that weekend. I explained that I was on retreat and that he could not see me. We arrived in time for supper but as usual I was not hungry and simply toyed with my meal. We were sleeping on campbeds in the hall next to the guest house. It was a freezing night and I was so cold that I felt physically sick. A friend gave me her blanket as she was warm but even so the cold crept deep into my bones.

I had been looking forward to going on retreat all term and the second day began well. We had a super talk on posture and prayer and then had our own little communion service in a tiny chapel in an old hermit's cell. We all went back to the guest house for coffee and sat singing folk songs to the guitar. Then we had lunch and just before the end I received a message that there was someone to see me. As I walked along the corridor my heart thumped. I hoped it was not my boyfriend; we had shared some happy moments and I did not want them to be destroyed. I opened the door and there he was. What on earth was I going to do? He had travelled about a hundred and fifty miles; how could I send him back straight away? I asked the RE teacher in charge if Andy could come to the university with us in the afternoon and to my relief he said he could. When we arrived back at the guest house I had to tell him to leave. I felt bad about the whole episode.

The following day was an absolute disaster. It was a Sunday and our last day on retreat. We walked to church and then returned to school by mini-bus. It was near to lunch-time when we arrived so we put our bags down outside the refectory and started to tell the others what it had been like. Matron came over and told me in a stern voice that the headmistress wanted to see me straightaway and that she was not in a very good mood. I knew it had to be something to do with the retreat weekend and I timidly walked into her office. It was. Everything had been blown up out of proportion. She said that when the RE teacher had reported Andy's appearance, I was the last person she had expected to be involved. I tried to tell her that I had spoken to Andy on the phone and told him not to come, but the tears surged forward. She said that she was shocked and what would my mother think.

She handed me a bus timetable and told me that I must catch the next bus to the city, walk to the guest house and apologise for having a male friend and being so rude. Then I must come straight back to school and apologise to the RE teacher and finally report back to her.

I was exhausted. Tears slowly trickled down my cheeks and I was shaking. As I was walking down the corridor I met Frances. She asked me what had happened and insisted that she came with me because I was in no fit state to go by myself and she was scared that I might get run over or collapse. I was so grateful to her for offering and she took my bags to the bedroom whilst I put a jacket on. There was a bitterly cold wind and we stood at the bus stop for ages, freezing. I had not got any gloves and was only wearing a fairly thin dress and jacket. Eventually we reached the guest house, and I knocked on the door. One of the sisters opened it.

"I am sorry," I said.

She asked me what I was sorry about and I explained the incident at the retreat. My eyes filled with tears and I was shivering with cold. She put her arm round me and said that she understood and I was not to worry about it. When she realised that we had come all that way she asked us to come inside and gave us some lunch. For once food felt really welcome. She told me to put everything in the past and take care going back to school.

When we arrived back I went and apologised to the RE teacher, who said he hoped I had learnt my lesson. I then reported to the headmistress. I was completely exhausted. I made my way to my bedroom, opened the door and collapsed on the floor. A friend came into the room and went to fetch one of the assistant matrons, Ann, who helped me on to my bed and put a blanket over me whilst she ran a hot bath. Afterwards she gave me an aspirin and made me lie down until supper-time.

"I'll pray for you, Helena," she said.

When the bell rang she told me I had better go into supper even if I did not eat anything, but I had better come back to bed straight afterwards. Later on in the evening I said that I wanted to ring home to wish my mother a

happy Mothers' Day. My mother asked how the retreat had
gone; I said that it was a disaster and told her what had
happened. I had been looking forward to that weekend all
term. I needed the spiritual strength, but the peace was
shattered. I forced back the tears as I explained about
having to go back to apologise, and how cold and ill I felt.
She was furious and upset that I had been treated this way
but unfortunately did not realise how ill I was, although
she rang the RE teacher to find out more and complain
about the harsh treatment. He said nothing whatsoever
about my physical state, commenting only that he had
given Andy permission to be with us and that his
behaviour and mine had been perfectly satisfactory. Not
surprisingly my mother did no more.

For the next two days I was still very ill and found it
almost impossible to concentrate on lessons. The thought
of the end of term being a few days away was the only thing
that kept me going. One evening the headmistress called
me to her office. She said that I looked very thin and pale,
that she had never seen anyone lose weight so quickly and
if I returned to school looking like this next term then she
would send me home straightaway. Then she went on to
ask me about how half-term had been and how my
grandparents were, whether I had heard from my mother
and how she was. It turned out to be a very pleasant chat
and she told me not to work too hard and make sure that I
ate.

In my last art lesson that term, I completed an
imaginative composition painting that I had been
working on for the past few weeks. The art teacher said
that it was very good and would I mind putting my name,
age and title on the back because she wanted to put it into
the Ellingham Mill art exhibition. I called the painting
"Inescapable Loneliness". I did not realise at the time that
a lot of my feelings had been reflected in this painting.
Lessons were coming to an end and the end of term spirit
set in. When the last night came a group of us wrapped
ourselves up in blankets to keep warm and watched the

academy awards in the television room, then we all
gathered in one bedroom and sat talking by torchlight.
Everyone kept on telling me that I looked terribly scrawny
and needed to put on weight. Two of the assistant matrons
walked in and said that they would turn a blind eye to the
fact that we were not in bed so long as we were a little
quieter. At about midnight they came in again and
suggested everyone went to bed.

We had the end of term eucharist and assembly and then
my father came to pick me up. I was so pleased to see him I
just wanted to get home as quickly as possible. He was
shocked at how ill I looked and remarked that I had lost a
lot of weight. My report was very good, and at the end the
headmistress said I had been working very hard and worn
myself into a shadow. When we arrived home my mother
was horrified at my appearance and feared that I had
leukaemia.

It was lovely to be home and in the warm.

My energy level was decreasing and I felt extremely
lethargic. During the day, whilst my parents were at work
and Ruth at college, I studied. One Saturday I wanted to
buy some more clothes and went into town with my
mother. She was really shocked at how thin I was when she
saw me undress. When we arrived back home I was so tired
that in the middle of one of my favourite television
programmes I went to bed. My mother came upstairs and
asked me why I was so tired. She thought it best to check on
what my weight was: I weighed six stone, ten pounds. I lay
down again, drained of energy. Her eyes filled with tears
and she voiced her regret at not being about to care for me
so far away at school, "I thought I was doing the right
thing."

To help me relax she gently massaged my back, but was
in for even more of a shock when she found that not only
were my arms and legs covered in hair but my back had a
line of fine body hair on it. My mother at that time knew
nothing of the symptoms of anorexia and though
saddened by the sight had no idea that it was linked with
my state of health.

We were meant to be going to Italy a few days later and my parents decided that I must see a doctor before we left. I went to a naturopathic doctor who gave me a medical check up, said that my liver was out of sorts and advised that I kept to a raw food diet. Ruth had finished the term at college and we were spending more time together and were far more compatible. The day before my parents and I were due to fly to Italy, while Ruth and I were sitting listening to records and talking, the telephone rang and she dashed to answer it. When she came back upstairs her eyes were watering and I knew there was something wrong. She told me that my grandfather was unconscious in hospital; he had suffered a heart attack. My parents came home and rang up to find out how he was – he was in a coma. The immediate reaction was to cancel our holiday, but we were all in need of one and knew that Grandad would want us to go and would be upset if we missed it because of him.

Early on Maundy Thursday we flew to Naples and travelled to Amalfi where we were to stay for a week. The scenery was beautiful and the change welcome. Good Friday brought a wonderful experience. In the evening all the houses and shops had fire torches outside; a procession of all white-hooded figures carrying a coffin came down the steps of the cathedral and through the streets; behind, there was a man in tatty clothes and bare feet carrying a cross – Jesus; following was a band and singers. The scene was very moving and I felt very close to God. We had a lovely time wandering around Pompei, going up Mount Vesuvius and visiting Capri. I was eating reasonably well but felt really cold the whole time. Towards the end of the holiday we received a telex to say that my grandfather had died on Good Friday night. My mother was obviously very upset at the loss of her father, but we knew that it was for the best.

We flew back to England ready to travel up to the cremation very early the next day. I had an appointment with the naturopathic doctor first, who was pleased that I had managed to maintain my weight whilst on holiday. He suspected that I had anorexia nervosa and put me on a special diet. Neither my parents nor I could believe that I had anorexia because I had not been slimming.

My grandfather's death was only the second I had known and I felt an inexplicable loss. I was not deeply upset, because death is something to be happy about, not sad, but I felt a strange emptiness. I helped arrange the flowers in the church and we had a beautiful requiem service and I knew that my grandfather was at peace.

I was due to return to school that week. My parents had already spoken to the headmistress and it had been decided that I would be a day girl, living with my grandmother so that she would have some company and I would be able to keep to the diet more easily. There had been so much tension during the past week it was difficult to eat even the smallest amount and food really nauseated me. I had dropped down to six and a half stone which was very little for my height. My mother was still staying the day I returned to school, and as it was a Friday, my half day, she planned to pick me up at the lunch break. I travelled in with Veronica, next-door, who taught at the junior house. I could not concentrate in lessons at all, if anyone asked me anything about the past I broke down, I was freezing cold and by the time my mother came I kept on having to go to the bathroom because of the laxatives that I had been given. I went back to my grandmother's and it was decided that I should have a second opinion over my symptoms.

I went along to a local GP who said that she wanted some blood and urine tests done at hospital. My mother drove me over to the hospital and sat with me whilst the blood was being taken. My pulse was weak and the doctor found it difficult to obtain any blood. He kept moving the needle further into my vein, suddenly my head felt heavy, I passed out. I did not know where I was when I first came round; I was lying flat, my mother and the doctor crouching over me. The nurse brought a glass of cold water and I stayed there a little longer before we drove back. I felt completely drained of all energy and my head still felt very heavy and dizzy. On the way we called in to see my friend Doris. She laid me down on the sofa by a warm log fire and brought some sweet lemon tea – my body craved sweetness in order to keep it going. It felt as though even the reserve glycogen supply in my muscles had been siphoned off.

The blood tests came through: I was a little anaemic but it was not leukaemia, which was a relief to everyone. However I was not well enough to return to school. It was decided that I would study at home and return only for the exams. I saw the teachers concerned who told me what to concentrate on. The cookery teacher very kindly rang up the Board to find out whether I could be assessed, so I left a medical certificate and some model answers in case they were of benefit. They all wished me a good recovery.

I worked on my studies at home, friends popped in to see me and I was reasonably content. I had no appetite whatsoever now, never felt hungry and constantly felt nauseated; still the weight dropped each day. I went to see my own doctor who sent me for blood tests and a chest X-ray. The blood tests proved negative, the lung fields appeared clear and there was no evidence of tuberculosis. When I returned to the doctor he said that he was referring me to a consultant physician at the Royal Berkshire Hospital. I was beyond caring now, I just wanted to find out what was wrong and to feel myself again. The days dragged on slowly; I began to feel that I could not go on much longer. At last the day to see the consultant physician came. He checked me over, asked a few questions about how I felt, then spoke to my parents and finally to me, saying that I had to drop O-levels and go into hospital to be treated for anorexia nervosa.

8

Never ending night

My life was in one hand,
I said, "let me fall or stand"
And with sadness did I speak
To feel so weak.

I prayed that the pain
Might soon wane,
As drifting in and out of sleep
Silent tears did I weep.

Until You entered my heart
Setting all fear apart,
And gave me the courage to fight
The never ending night.

I hold my heart in my hand,
Before God's face I stand,
All love I have, I bring;
Unto You do I sing.

At 9.30 a.m. on Thursday, May 15th 1980, I was admitted to the Royal Berkshire Hospital. I had previously been told that I was being sent to the medical ward which nursed people with various diseases. I imagined a room with perhaps ten beds, people of my age and a little older, a day room with a television and a chance for visitors to come and sit peacefully and chat. The room would be clean and clinical with a tranquil atmosphere, only the murmur of nurses' voices and tapping of feet along the corridors. I think my notion was misguided, as from the minute I was admitted things were not in the least as I had expected. I was taken past a row of beds occupied by motionless bodies, the smell of illness oozing around my heavy head. I found myself in a room isolated from the rest of the ward.

Before I had a chance to be accustomed to my new accommodation, I had to change into my nightclothes, and sit on the weighing scales. I watched a graph being pinned above my bed which I presumed was to monitor the progress or decline, as the case may be, of my weight. There certainly was no delay in the arrival of the doctor. My parents were asked to leave and I was left with the doctor and the nurse who had just weighed me. The door was closed, the windows shut and the light above my bed switched on. He proceeded to open up his case. I feared the worst and wished I could disappear. I was not in the mood to be poked and prodded around. First they took a standing up blood pressure, then a lying down blood pressure. Whilst lying down they drained more blood out of me, took my temperature and pulse, along with a few other tests, spoke some medical jargon and told me I would be visited by another doctor in a short while.

At midday I was served a plateful of half-cold food covered by a metal lid, which I cautiously lifted up. The drifting smell that escaped made me feel sick and I just pushed it aside. Shortly afterwards the dietician paid me a visit, clutching a clipboard with various pieces of paper attached. She looked down at one of the sheets of paper and explained that everything I ate had to be carefully recorded and the calorific value for each day worked out, increasing the calories to between two and three thousand per day. I was to be put on a high-protein, high-calorie diet as the energy available from my previous diet was insufficient to meet demands and the amino-acids were being used a source of energy, as opposed to their correct use of building new body tissue and controlling chemical changes within the body cells. If this were prolonged it could have adverse effects upon the blood and vital body organs. She went on to mention that ideally she would like an hourly feed of "build-ups", a milk-based liquid.

It was not long before one of the nurses came along with a bedpan and asked for a urine sample, then confidently went ahead with taking my temperature, pulse and blood pressure again. I had only been in hospital for five hours, yet I had already begun to feel like a test-dummy – things constantly pumped in and out! The consultant physician came along and talked for a short time, mentioning that I would be put on a phenothiazine drug, chlorpromazine, otherwise known as largactil. It is a sedative which is supposed to enhance the appetite and prevent nausea and vomiting. Either largactil or insulin is used when treating anorexia. The physician said that he would be visiting me once a week on the doctor's rounds, but one of several house-doctors would be checking up on me daily.

"Peace at last!" I thought to myself in the evening. I was absolutely exhausted and in desperate need of some sleep. However, I discovered even on the first night that sleeping for any length of time in a hospital is an almost impossible task. I fell asleep directly my head hit the pillow, despite the noise and the fact that the lights were blazing, but the next thing I was aware of was being woken up by a stranger. It was the staff nurse with the medicine trolley of all things! Trying to sleep again was hopeless: the crashing and banging from the sluice, ambulance sirens in the distance and various unidentifiable noises swirled around my throbbing head. What is more I was freezing cold and can never get to sleep when cold. So I became restless, trying to find a position in which I could best conserve the heat, blot out the noise and at the same time try to think pleasant thoughts to take my mind off the depressing surroundings. Presumably aroused by my restlessness there was soon a nurse at my bedside.

"Are you all right, love?"

I looked at the shadowy figure beside my bed. I could just make out her face by the light thrown on it, shining through the gap in the door.

"I can't sleep and I'm cold," I whispered. She fetched me another blanket and sat and talked for a while. Then I fell asleep.

The following morning I was woken up at 6.00 a.m. to be given a cup of tea. My first reaction was annoyance. I could not understand why I was not left to sleep. However, I felt consoled when the same nurse as last night came and talked to me until the changeover shift. Naturally the starting conversation had to be my illness. She mentioned that previously there had been a little girl suffering from the same disease on this ward who walked out a happy girl, full of life, but it took a couple of months of intensive treatment. I could not help but think, "I only hope I don't have to be in this room for a couple of months, it would be unbearable." The subject, to my relief, soon changed to hobbies and interests, and we discovered that we shared a love of dancing.

As the sun rose it shone on the flower poster I had beside me, lighting up its delicate petals. I read a few pages from the book *Appointment in Jerusalem*★ and was actually

★*Appointment in Jerusalem* by Derek Prime, Kingsway Publications convinced there was good to be derived from bad. This idea did not last long though. I was suddenly gripped by an overwhelming sense of loneliness. My light which I had tried to keep burning became shaded by darkness which extended into a thick grey cloud.

The hours blurred into days. I was still isolated in that small room surrounded only by four walls. The routine of having my blood pressure, temperature, pulse and weight recorded became monotonous. I was managing to take some solid food, but it continued to nauseate me and my weight still fell. I could not read more than one page of a book without my concentration being impaired. If I were to stand for long I felt drastically heavy-headed and faint due to the high dosage of largactil three times a day. I began to live only for the visitors who came to see me. They were the highlights of my day, but my lack of concentration made it difficult for people to stay long.

After about a week of being separated from other patients I was taken into the adjoining ward to make room for a woman with an undiagnosed disease requiring complete isolation. I walked alongside the sister into the large ward. Everyone was a lot older than me and I felt very uneasy. The sister showed me to my new bed, number 27, quite by coincidence the same number as the cot in the hospital where I had been born!

A little while later a young girl of fifteen, only a year younger than me, was admitted into the next bed. I soon discovered that she was called Helen. We began to exchange information about our illnesses. For several months she had repeatedly suffered from fevers, headaches and weakness. It had been put down as glandular fever, but she was brought into hospital for further investigation.

My first night in the ward was terrible, far noisier than the previous room, and the moaning of ill people was most disconcerting. I lay awake watching the nurses check up on the glucose drips at odd times, observed them changing the bags for the lady next to me who was having a blood transfusion and watched other people being taken off or put on saline drips. There appeared to be more activity at night than in the day.

Having had such an unrestful night I woke up feeling even more tired. I don't think Helen had had much sleep either.

"Is it always as distracting as that during the night?" she asked. "And do they have to wake you up at 6.30 a.m.?"

"'Fraid so!" I replied. "In a few minutes the auxiliaries will come round with a bowl of water and draw the curtains round your bed so that you can wash."

Sure enough they did. We were shut off from one another by curtains but that did not prevent us from carrying on our conversation. It was a real consolation to find someone else whose O-levels were having to suffer due to illness. Helen was not quite as unfortunate as I was as she was not in her O-level year, but the subjects she was taking early had to be forgotten. I had taken three early, but the remaining five and four CSEs had been ruled out. In expressing our anguish over such matters we both felt a lot better.

After breakfast the same house-doctor whom I had seen when first admitted paid me a visit. He was young and much easier to talk to than a lot of the other doctors. "He has a good bedside manner," as one of the nurses put it.

As he approached the end of my bed he looked at my medical file, then peered up at my weight chart.

"Hey, your weight chart is going the wrong way. I wouldn't like to see you fall off the bottom!"

He looked down at me and smiled, then walked round to the side of my bed. He turned to the chart again, "You know when you come out of hospital you ought to paint that chart; it looks rather like mountains, don't you think?"

I nodded my head, feeling rather amused at the thought. He sat down on the edge of my bed and looked at me with sincerity. I dreaded what his next words would be, since my weight had fallen.

"Last time I came to see you, you had been drawing a picture. Have you done any more?"

Relief swept over me and I passed him my latest sketch book.

"They're lovely," he said, glancing through the pages. "If you are this good now, with extra tuition you could make a good position in the art world."

I felt quite touched by his last remark.

In the afternoon the same doctor was on his rounds and happened to walk past my bed; he glanced at my weight chart quickly.

"That's more like it," he said, "It's looking more like a mountain now!"

He smiled and carried on with his rounds.

I could hardly believe my ears. My weight had increased by only 0.2 kg, yet he had bothered to comment and even shown enthusiasm. I was half expecting some sarcastic comment like, "It's meant to be a mountain not a molehill."

I actually managed to eat something, only I had such an excruciating pain in my stomach that I began to wonder whether the effort was really worth the pain and discomfort. I desperately needed reassurance but the following day the hammer came down with a mighty blow. Once again I had slept badly, had woken up with a crashing headache and feeling considerably weaker. Throughout the day I felt worse and by the afternoon I had gone down quite a lot in weight. I had not had my bowels open for five days so experienced an unpleasant and unsuccessful suppository, followed by a bowel enema. When the staff nurse explained what this was I tried to put off having it as I felt so weak. I simply could not bear the thought of any painful treatment, but I had to go ahead with feeling degraded and having the last of my energy siphoned out.

No sooner were the curtains drawn back than one of the less pleasant house-doctors came to see me. He promptly sat down on my bed and looked up at my weight chart in a scornful manner. "Why have you lost weight?" was his first question, asked in a harsh, penetrating voice. He was incredibly tactless about my condition and I felt a lump form in my throat. He stood up and briskly drew the curtains around my bed. His hurtful comments continued to shower me and he forced me to drink every drop of the soup that was in my hand. Finally he got up and walked away, leaving the curtains still around me.

Emotionally, I was too weak to cope, I felt my body tense up, slowly tears rolled down my cheeks. A few minutes later nurse C peeped round the curtain. She was a very caring and competent person and I got on well with her. She rushed over to my bed.

"What did he say to you?" she said with compassion.

I told her all that the house-doctor had said , that they would stop even visitors coming to see me if I didn't get better soon and how he had made me drink the soup in front of him.

"Take no notice whatsoever; he hasn't got much patience for this illness I'm afraid."

At last they put an end to my restless nights. The nurses had noticed that I had not been sleeping and the physician prescribed sleeping tablets. Whilst visiting me, he had voiced his concern as I had lost even more weight that day. My bones felt extra prominent as they rubbed against the sheets and became sore. For the first time I was able to see that I was thin. The nurse had left the bathroom for a few minutes, and on looking in the mirror I saw my whole hip-joint, the rounded bone from my front to my back, but it did not worry me in the least.

The sleeping pills had worked wonders the previous night, but the second night I did not sleep quite so peacefully. I was knocked out five minutes after taking the pills but woke up several times after that. I saw the night sister being taken round the beds by one of the SRN nurses, who informs her of each patient's illness and progress. I had been awake on several occasions when they had walked past before. The nurse would whisper something about me to the sister, who nodded her head and said, "Hello", recognising that I was awake. This particular night I decided that I had better pretend to be asleep, after all I was on sleeping pills! As I lay there, my eyes closed and my breathing shallow, they approached the end of my bed.

"This is Helena, a little anorexic girl. She has been in for several weeks now and has continued to decline. Her condition is serious and they are fighting for her."

What I had just heard was certainly not what I had expected to hear. I knew I was ill, but was unaware that it had got to that extreme. I was so desperately confused. It was not that I did not want to get better, I just could not get better. I lay there terrified, my emotions knotted up. I honestly did not know which was the best alternative: to try to cope with fighting the battle, or to be defeated.

I went up in weight by 100g the following day and the doctors mentioned that they were aiming for my weight to reach 42 kg before they decided whether I was well enough to leave hospital. I looked up at the graph. I was not much good with metric weight and roughly converted it into imperial – it was about six and a half stone. I felt disillusioned. It seemed miles to the top of that graph, and surely an impossibility to reach it within the next few weeks. It seemed such a long time till I would be coming out. Even if I managed to put the weight on quickly I still did not feel cured within myself and I would only have a relapse and find myself back in there. I wanted to get better, yet at the same time was afraid of getting better; why, I don't know. I was in a dark tunnel and I did not know which end had the most light; which way should I turn?

I lay there feeling miserable and dejected. The days passed by, marked only by the recurring discomfort of the pain in my stomach and the unease of the monotonous position in bed. My weight had gone up slightly one day but it could not last and the next day I had lost twice the amount. I was totally humiliated. Nurse C came over to take my blood pressure and pulse. She looked at me with deep concern in her eyes.

"I am really worried about you now, you're only five and a half stone. Young girls of your age have died of anorexia and I hope to God you don't."

I was stunned; I did not know what to say.

That night something happened that radically changed my perception of myself and gave me the courage to fight. I had fallen asleep a short time before the medicine trolley came round and consequently woke up in the middle of the night feeling severely depressed. I tossed and turned for several hours, crying quietly to myself. I felt isolated and lonely; I could not bear to be awake any longer experiencing these terrible feelings. I rang my bell; the nurse soon arrived.

"Can I have my sleeping pills please? I can't sleep," I asked.

"Sorry, it's gone midnight and we can't issue them after this time," she replied.

As she walked away tears flooded down my sunken cheeks; I could not face any more. My body felt icy cold and as though it was sinking deeper, deeper.

I felt that the little life within me was being drained from my body and the hands of Death were firmly gripping me. I had no more strength to fight, no will to live. All I could do was pray to God that His will for me should be done. At that moment I just surrendered to Him the little life that was left and said, "Lord, if you want me to die, I'll die, but if you want me to live then give me the courage to fight this illness and live."

I was wide awake and very aware of all that was going on around me. As I looked across at the curtains closed round the bed opposite, I saw the faint figure of a young woman radiating beauty and tranquillity. Her smile warmed my heart and the kindness in her eyes filled me with a strange love and peace. Suddenly my body felt warm and relaxed. I turned over and switched on my tape of Fisherfolk songs and the words which came singing into my ears were,

"Jesus took my burdens and rolled them in the sea." I knew instantly that I had been promised life.

I sat up and wiped my eyes. One of the nurses came over to me and asked, "Do you want a drink?"

"Yes please, I'll have a cup of Horlicks."

I could not believe what I had just said. I had asked for a milky drink and for the first time I actually drank it all, closed my eyes and fell asleep.

A real flood of joy had entered my heart that night; I knew that the missing piece to the puzzle of my life had been discovered. I felt an inexplicable love and security. I had previously been a Christian and needed God to help me gain self-confidence and find a purpose in the things I did, but it was all out of focus. I called upon God when I personally needed Him to help me cope with my inabilities; now I began to see that my life had circulated around my own values, ideas and ego. I had misconceived the fact that Jesus suffered on the Cross to save the lives of others.

After the previous night's terrifying yet wonderful experience, I began the day praising God. I was inspired to eat and I did, but was over-enthusiastic. I was sick and had a tremendous pain; I lay quietly sobbing.

At visiting time when my mother walked in I was sitting up in bed. I was so full of my amazing experience that I hardly let her reach the bed before I said, "Mum, I've got something to tell you," and proceeded to describe the events of the previous night and my over-enthusiastic attempts to eat during the day.

She then said, "Right, now I can tell you what happened to me last night. I was so desperately worried that you had lost the will to live that I could not settle to sleep and busied myself sorting things in my room. I picked up my little statue of the Virgin Mary to dust it and move it nearer to my bed. In the agony of my despair I sat on the bed and did something I have never done before. Holding the little figure in my hands I prayed, 'Mary, you know what it is like to see your child suffer and die; please pray to your Son for my child.' It seems the prayer was answered in a very special way."

The pain in my stomach became so great with the effort of increased eating, like a rupture at times, my skin dry; my arms, legs and back had excessive fine hair growing and my head hair was moulting rapidly, I felt so degraded, I began to feel, "Why bother?" Then I read in the magazine *Every day with Jesus*, "Many people these days give up too easily. One harsh word of criticism, one lost battle in the war, and they lose heart and enthusiasm."

After reading that, I decided that however difficult it may be I was not going to be defeated by a callous disease such as anorexia nervosa. It might be a very difficult disease to overcome but I made up my mind that I was not going to take the "why bother" attitude. I was going to fight it through to the end and cling on to my faith.

At this stage in my life I came to know a man from the Salvation Army. He had bright eyes and was a bouncy little fellow, who kept sending super letters to try to cheer me up. He would begin by saying, "Hello Cheerie Cherub." On this particular occasion he enclosed some jokes and a fifty-pence piece. His letters were so amusing and often cheered me up when I was in pain or feeling low.

9

On the water's edge

My body's a piece of seaweed
On the water's edge,
It rises and falls
With the tide.

The lashing waves tear me
On the jagged rocks,
They throw me up high
And beat me down.

A rejected lifeless weed
Swept on to the shore,
Helplessly I shrivel up
In the burning sun.

Throw me back into the sea,
Help me feel the water
Pass into my body
And give me life.

The days ticked on; my weight had both its ups and downs. Each day I benefited in as much as I learnt about other people's difficulties. I began to see the similarities in struggling towards normal health between my illness and other illnesses. Within the same ward there were people suffering from overweight problems, cancer and overdose cases. I got on well with one woman in particular who had taken an overdose. She often looked at the illustrated diary that I kept, and I think the short spell in hospital faced with people struggling to live whilst she had tried to take her life gave her the will to live again. There were several patients who had had strokes and a few with lung complications, one of whom was about a year younger than me. We played chess together and sat and talked, mostly about dancing.

The only difference between the other patients and me was that they came and went and I stayed. The only other person who had been there as long as I had was Winnie. She was trying to lose weight but the process was complicated by her being in a wheelchair. She would often zoom along to my bed and chat for half an hour. She mentioned a woman a couple of beds away, Mary, whom she thought I might like to meet. I ambled along to see her and almost immediately we became great friends. I benefited through her experiences as she did through mine. Her problem was that she kept on becoming anaemic and the doctors were puzzled as to where the blood was going. There were no signs of her passing blood from anywhere, yet a few days after each transfusion she became cold and pale; the blood had mysteriously disappeared.

The days continued to add up. I was slowly progressing,

my head began to feel a little lighter and I could appreciate each day's happenings. I was actually becoming aware of everyday life; it was like stepping out of a cloud. My weight was creeping up but I still was not hungry, as if the gastric juices were refusing to churn, and I looked upon food with disgust. I was improving but I was still still frightened and confused. The weighing scales continued to confront and accost me; I wished they would just go away. It seemed as though they ruled my life.

"Why can't you just leave my weight alone?" I asked nurse G in desperation.

"We can't afford to, Helena, it could have fatal effects upon your kidneys, liver or blood. I know it's difficult but you must try to help us. Why not try to take one thing at a time, eat something you would not normally have as a sacrifice for someone else?"

"Okay, I'll try. But I just can't face it; I don't want anything and I feel so pressurised," I replied.

"Don't try to face a meal, just take a little and often. But don't be put off by a meal; if you can't face it eat at least a little and then if you feel hungry later I'll always bring you something along."

"Yes," I replied hesitantly and not too convinced.

"Listen, you like strawberries and raspberries don't you?"

"Yes."

"Well, why not try a little milk on them? It won't make a lot of difference but it will just give you a few more nutrients."

I felt a little more encouraged; nurse G was so understanding and gentle, with a non-pressurising attitude.

Shortly afterwards the dietitian came. "Hello, Helena, how are you feeling?"

"All right, thanks," I replied.

"Let's have a look at the chart," she said glancing up at the weight graph and then down at her calculations. "Oh dear, I think I would like the liquid build-ups increased.

Without that the calories are only in the hundreds, not between two and three thousand. How do you feel about it?"

"I don't want the build-ups increased," I admitted. I didn't particularly like them.

"The more it is increased, the more your weight goes up. Perhaps the nurses could give it to you between each meal."

I felt disheartened but agreed just for the sake of peace. Then she mentioned that my haemoglobin count was low and that she wanted me to receive more iron.

Next, one of the doctors, quite out of the blue, came over to me and said that he would like my stomach looked at after a meal. He gave no explanation as to why he wanted it to be looked at and how the doctors would do this. I was left in the dark. I knew the doctors were only trying to do their best, so it was not having my stomach looked at that scared me but the fact that the illness was such a mystery. In many ways I longed to be happy and healthy, yet there was something preventing me from wanting to get better. As well as the sight and smell of food nauseating me terribly, I was terrified of putting on weight. It is a situation that can only be fully understood by sufferers of anorexia nervosa themselves because it is so obscure. I am sure that most people must find it very difficult to understand why anorexics resist putting on weight; they are emaciated and quite obviously the first stage of recovery is to increase their weight. It sounds so simple, but having to force food down when even the sight of it is enough to nauseate one is not easy. Then there is the fear that whatever one eats leads to an increase in weight, and the terrifying feeling that in gaining one pound, then one stone, will lead to never being able to stop putting weight on. This is complicated further by anorexics not being able to see how thin they are. Instead, when they look into the mirror they visualise a body covered in fat; not even flesh, but fat.

I felt very low-spirited, probably because of being told

that the liquid build-ups had to be increased. With the amount of calories that were going into me daily I felt like a pig being fattened for eating. It was a horrible feeling, but when I tried to escape it I felt trapped. I was stuck in a maze, lost and confused, my life surrounded by paths leading to dead ends. I followed one after another desperately trying to find an escape. There was no escape; there was no end. "Is life worth living if there's no end to my misery?" I thought to myself. "No, it isn't."

I thought of Mrs T who had died of cancer that day. She was a wonderful person; her faith so deep, her courage so strong. She fought her illness to the end despite the tremendous pain and the knowledge that she was dying.

Mrs T and I had both found great comfort in the Wednesday ward communions. Before breakfast the chaplain would set up a little altar in the centre. It was a beautiful and peaceful time. There was also a small chapel downstairs which my mother and I had attended on the first Sunday but not since. One Sunday, though, Mary, the woman who kept losing blood, suggested we go to the service together. It was a lovely idea and Sister allowed Mary to have breakfast by my bed before we went down. One of the nurses assisted us down the stairs as we were so weak. The service was beautiful and moved both of us greatly.

Afterwards there were no nurses to help us back and we must have looked funnier than any comedians, helping each other up the stairs in our nightclothes.

I desperately needed the strength the communion had given me on the following day when I was faced with a barium meal and x-ray.

At 11.30 p.m. on the Sunday, one of the nurses brought me a drink and pinned a notice above my bed. I twisted round to read it, half expecting it to say, "For Sale", but it said "Nil after midnight."

As usual I was woken up at 6.30 a.m. At breakfast-time I was quite content that I was not allowed anything to eat. The next few hours were simply anticipation as I sat and waited. One of the nurses gave me a white gown to change into, then a porter arrived and wrapped me up in a red blanket and wheeled me down to the x-ray department. I waited, quietly watching out-patients come and go. I heard my name called. "Helena Wilkinson." A nurse collected my notes and wheeled me into a dimly-lit room filled with large metal equipment.

"Hello Helena," the doctor said. He gave me twenty white pills to swallow with two sips of water, a not too difficult feat. He then produced a carton of emulsion-like liquid with a straw. This had to be sipped at intervals, when directed, once I was on the x-ray table. The mass of equipment was most impressive and I was gently tilted back into a horizontal position, looking up at the metal monsters above me. Every now and then, as I held the white liquid in my mouth the command to "swallow" came. A television screen lit up and when the x-ray was switched on I saw my insides appear on the screen. This was repeated several times and then I was turned on my side. The hip bones of my emaciated body ground into the metal; my limbs turned blue with cold.

How thankful I was when the performance was finished. The porter wheeled me back to bed and handed my notes to Sister. I felt terrible and just lay exhausted, huddled on my bed in my white gown and still wrapped in the red blanket. But there was to be no peace that day. In no time there was beside me a woman in a white overall. I glanced at the needle in her hand.

"Not more blood," I said.

"Yes, more blood."

I pulled my lifeless body up the bed and placed my arm in front of her. She slid the needle in, nothing happened, she pushed it still further. I felt incredibly sick.

"Your veins are rather small and your pulse weak. Let's try the other arm."

Reluctantly I gave her the other arm. In slid the needle; I felt myself drifting off and groaned. She laid me down as I went out. Unbelievably, when I came round she said,

"Right love, we'll give it one more try."

I felt drained and I lay motionless for the rest of that day. I cannot remember eating anything and the only time I was moved was for weighing, still lying wrapped up in the red blanket.

In the afternoon the physician came and told me that the x-ray had shown no blockage but my stomach had shrunk severely and needed to be stretched. I suppose it was quite a relief but at that moment I could not have cared what news he brought. He admitted that they were not having great success with me, and said that he was calling in the aid of a child psychiatrist.

I don't remember anything else about that day except that when my mother came to visit me after school I was still lying huddled on my bed in the x-ray gown.

She brought with her a shaft of sunlight. After she had helped me back into my nightclothes we prayed together, as we did every night of my stay in hospital. They were simple, straightforward prayers; clasping my hand in hers in a sign of unity of purpose and caring, we would pray for the doctors and nurses, the other patients, sometimes specifically by name, and lastly for me. This night in particular these prayers gave me back my strength, my peace and the determination not to let my faith slide.

10

Hidden tears

As for me
I dream of how
Life used to be;
The people for whom
I cared,
For the memories
I shared.

Hidden tears
Behind my eyes
Reveal the fears
Which my mind
Now knows;
Such pain my body
Shows.

But every day
I quietly sit
And pray
For other's pain
I see,
Thanking God for the good
In me

One day one of the staff nurses helped me along to a little room outside the ward to see two of the team of child psychiatrists who had been called in. The strangest thing was shaking hands with two men whilst dressed in my nightclothes. I perched on the edge of the chair, while one of the doctors told me exactly what anorexia nervosa is and the effects it can have upon you. Then they began to ask questions about my past history. They seemed very nice people, and to my surprise I soon began to feel at ease. They appeared very concerned that after a long spell in hospital I had not really shown any sign of improvement. One of them asked to see my arms; I pulled up my sleeve in response.

"Look, what d'you think?" he said to the other man.

"Yes, it is quite bad," he replied.

"Can you lean forward a minute, love, so that we can look at the top of your back."

I leant forward; he pulled my dressing-gown away from my neck.

"Yes," he sighed, "It's pretty serious."

They explained that the lanugo (fine hair) that appeared especially on the arms, and in extreme cases down the back and around the face, was one of the features of anorexia. They asked if I had it on my legs, especially my thighs; I admitted I had and felt degraded by it.

"We are going to put you on complete bed rest; that means you can't get up for anything at all."

That would not make a vast amount of difference, just that there would be no more physiotherapy and I would depend on my bell a lot more!

"We will also try increasing the largactil to 75 mg three times a day."

Sounds like I am back at square one, I thought to myself.

"We are sending someone along to talk to you once a week. She's a child psychiatrist and she'll see you and your parents together first and then you by yourself."

I was not very enthusiastic about the idea, but went along with it.

"I'll be going along to talk to your parents within the next few days and we'll see how things go from there."

I said goodbye and found my own way back to the ward.

Back in the ward I could take stock of how bedrest would affect me. To lose the physiotherapy seemed partly good and partly bad. Early on the doctor had wanted me to have exercises and so had asked my mother to take me swimming. A good friend who was headmistress of a local school allowed us to use the swimming pool after the girls had finished. It was lovely to get out of hospital but I was so weak I had almost to learn to swim again.

For some strange reason the doctors then stopped this happy outing and changed me to hospital physiotherapy which was less pleasant. Whether they thought it would help to strengthen my muscles more quickly, I don't know, but I exchanged my contact with the outside world for a burgundy tracksuit and the dreariness of the hospital gymnasium. There was a hard board to lie on, straps on my legs and bean-bags, which increased in weight each day, on my ankles. Every day, with increasing weakness, after weight-loss and extra exercise I felt more and more exhausted. I was therefore not sorry to say goodbye to physiotherapy for the moment.

Unfortunately, I was not the only person who had become worse. My friend, Mary, suddenly haemorrhaged badly and was rushed to another ward. I thought about her a lot. She was a splendid example of courage. We kept in touch through my mother or the newspaper boy. One morning I received a letter from her that meant a tremendous amount to me.

Dear Helena,
    I've been thinking of you quite a lot since I left the

ward on Friday. The little text did help, and it came along with another little miracle which I'll have to tell you or your mother about. I'm not like you dear, I don't express myself very well on paper.

Like me I hear that you're confined to your bed, so I only hope it's having a good effect on you dear; it is on me. I am still too sore to want to move around much, but now that my drip is off my arm and the tubes out of my nose I'm feeling better all the time.

Sunday morning at communion time I thought about our going down together the Sunday before. I'm so glad we made it; I was able to go through it all in my head. Well, love, I'm having breakfast this morning, my first food since last Thursday so I'm ready for it, and it's just going on the rounds. I want Ivor the paper boy to be postman for me so it will have to be cheerio for now.

Don't give up your fighting spirit, Helena, I know with the help of Jesus you will beat this illness. I can see your name in print, for I'm sure that one day you will be famous. This spell in hospital also has its purpose of making you aware of your own capabilities, and it's an experience that God must want you to have. Unpleasant though it may be now, I'm sure that soon it will be all behind you. So God bless you dear, I shall never forget the pleasure of knowing you. I hope to get up to see you all in "Adelaide" soon.

Love Mary

The miracle that she mentioned in her letter was that she had received the laying on of hands by a pastor, and the blood that she had been given had not disappeared. If everything was well after several days then she could go home. It was; the blood stayed and no further transfusion was needed – it was incredible. I had not been happier in weeks when I heard that she could definitely go home in a few days' time. It certainly was a miracle.

I just kept praying to God that He would help me to overcome this illness and lose my profound fear, but it was more than I could cope with; I became depressed and began to cry. I was lost in a terrifying world, fear just ran through my blood, my body became flushed as the tears trickled down my drab face.

"Don't worry."

I peered up through my tear-stricken eyes and saw Nurse G sympathetically looking down at me. She drew the curtains round my bed and sat down.

"You don't want all those people watching do you?"

"No," I mumbled, trying to hold back the tears.

"Have a cry if you want, Helena, you've had to put up with a lot recently, and now you can't move from your bed for anything. I think that's really unfair."

"So do I, it's really degrading having to use a bed-pan and not being able to do anything without a nurse there. I can't bear it any longer."

I felt the lump in my throat get bigger, I swallowed hard and bit my lip.

"Have lots of milky drinks."

The thought repulsed me, tears surged forward. "I hate milk," I said sharply.

"Oh dear! You were drinking it quite a lot at one time and your weight was going up, now it's below six stone again."

"I can't drink milk any more," I said.

"I know it's difficult, Helena, but people have won through, and you must try. So many people don't understand just what a fight it is, but you believe in God, don't you?"

"Yes, that's the only thing that's stopped me from giving up," I replied.

"Well, don't give up please."

We sat chatting for a while; then she left me. She had given me the reassurance that I so desperately needed at that moment. I knew that I must not give up as I looked at two girls in nearby beds who had taken overdoses; they had tried to take their own lives, because they were unable to face the future. If I gave up now, I would be doing exactly the same, I would be taking an easy way out of facing my problems. Yet before Nurse G spoke to me and so many times in the past, I wished that I did not exist. The endless depressions and the grip of the disease were mental torture, and the simplest way to put an end to it was to put an end to life. I knew I could not do this; I had to persevere.

During one of the visiting times when my mother was with me, the child psychiatrist came. I was very weak and did not feel like talking; however, I complied. Her questions were very personal and I felt incredibly awkward when she asked my mother about her marriage in front of me. Unfortunately she just was not the right person to help me, she brought back painful memories. I know that is what psychiatry is concerned with, but she made no attempt to heal it. Each time I saw her she mentioned that she wanted me to go to the hospital where she worked but first I would have to reach six and a half stone. She said there would be other young people, with similar and different problems; there would be a lot of activity going on; there would also be medical staff keeping an eye on my condition. At one point she almost convinced me that it would be a good idea, that I would have friends of my own age, I would not be stuck in a hospital bed all day and I would benefit by hearing other people's problems as well as discussing my own. Then I realised I would be in an institution, a hospital environment, a psychiatric hospital at that, for weeks, possibly months, surrounded only by young people, some with a lot worse problems than mine. I would doubtless go from better to worse. There would be little hope for the future, my career prospects ruined. Valuable years of my life would be lost by simply dwelling on my illness and being bound by the past – what a ghastly thought.

I had been confined to bed for several weeks when one day there was a break in the monotony. In the morning we had the ward service which was an inspiration for the rest of the day for several of us. Then I had two surprise visitors, a Sister from a nearby convent school who was very kind, and Helen, the girl who had been in the next bed

several weeks back. It was great to see her again and hear
all her news. She brought me some beautiful sweet peas
from her garden which brightened my corner up. It had
been a long time since we had seen one another and we
chatted for quite some time until my father came in. I felt
quite exhausted after having three visitors in succession.

In the afternoon I heard some of the student nurses
talking about a fire practice. Then one said to me, "You're
on complete bedrest aren't you?"

"Yes. What's going on?" I replied.

"Oh, we're going to have a fire practice throughout the
hospital. Those on complete bedrest are either left in bed
or carried in a blanket or stretcher and other patients are
assisted down the fire escapes. It's just so that we can carry
out the practical procedures," she explained.

"What will happen to me then?" I asked.

"I don't know, Sister will tell you."

I was all for drama. It looked like a bit of fun as I
watched the nurses practise carrying each other in
blankets as a stretcher. Then the sister came over.

"Hello, Helena. You don't want to miss out on the fun
do you?"

"No!" I replied in an enthusiastic voice.

"Well, I'll let one of the student nurses accompany you
to the edge of the fire escape."

I was so pleased I could join in the fun and have the
opportunity to get out of bed. A first-year student nurse
came along and helped me to the fire escape; my legs felt as
though they had seized up and were very weak. I shuffled
along to the door; as I approached it fresh air whirled
around my head, sweet-smelling summer air, birds
singing and the sun warm and shining brightly. It
brought an immediate feeling of joy and beauty to my
heart. I took a deep breath and sighed heavily. Sister had
told me to go only as far as the door, but the nurse
proceeded to take me down the stairs out into the open. I
presumed Sister had changed her mind so I made every
effort to go. Besides, the fresh air was so welcoming that I

was prepared to push myself, but it was a struggle to get back up to the top again; I was exhausted.

The following day was unfortunately rather more than just an anti-climax. I can only presume it happened because of the previous day's activities. I was woken up at 6.00 a.m., shortly after which the staff nurse came to take my blood pressure. They always took two readings, one lying, the other standing. I did not know a lot about blood pressure except that mine was well below normal. The nurse wound the strip around my arm and began to pump.

"We don't seem to be doing too well today, I can't get a reading."

She paused for a while. "Ah yes, here we are."

She scribbled down some figures and asked me to stand up. I promptly pushed the bedclothes aside and stood beside the bed. She wound the strip around my arm and once more began to pump. I suddenly felt incredibly sick and shuffled back a few paces to prop my body up against the bed to give me the extra security. The strip around my arm deflated.

"I don't seem to be able to get a reading this time either," she said in a rather concerned voice.

I thought to myself, please don't try again, just let me lie down.

"I'll try again," she said.

Only this time she pumped it up a little tighter. I felt the blood rush from my head, the warm liquid flowed down my body, once more I felt incredibly sick, as though my head was clamped between metal tongs.

"Help! I'm going," I mumbled.

The nurse rang my bell and immediately another nurse arrived. They lifted me on to the bed, drew the curtains round and began to wind the handle at the end to raise the bottom of my bed. The last thing I remember before I went out was, "Call the night sister quick."

When I came round it was amazingly peaceful; the curtains were still drawn around my bed, but the sun was streaming in through the window. My feet were still much higher than my head, it was a strange sensation. I do not know what happened whilst I was out; all I could remember was the bustle that took place beforehand. I lay in that position for quite some time before I asked one of the nurses if I could be lowered. The blood had re-entered my head but I felt incredibly weak and drained of all energy. The staff nurse came along and lowered my bed when she was on the rounds with the medicine trolley. I just lay there, mesmerised, until my mother came at visiting-time. I think the news was rather a shock to her, but she was very good with her courage and support, as were many people. I do not think anything could have replaced those small touches of friendship that brought reassurance.

After my parents had gone in the evening, I had an extreme wave of depression; every minute seemed an hour long and I wished I could drop off to sleep and wake up completely better, as though the entire illness had been a bad dream. At times I even believed I was having a bad dream and that I would soon wake up and forget it all, once again enjoying myself in everyday activities. "Everyday activities," I thought to myself, "they are non-existent at the moment and will probably remain that way for a long time." All the memories of the sports I participated in at school came flooding back, the tremendous sensation of one's body flying through the air after a neck spring, the mystique of tap dancing; I could not bear to think of these any more, my eyes filled with tears. It was a vicious circle, too vicious, and I was just going round and round it, being torn to shreds.

The night staff had just come on duty and were going round each bed, sliding the head rest into the sleeping position and shaking up the pillows. I saw one of the auxiliaries coming in my direction: she was ever such a sweet woman, so gentle and caring. I closed my tear-stained eyes in haste.

"Hello, poppet." she said in her usual cheery voice.

I did not reply. I thought it better not to, for I knew that if I were to open my mouth I would burst into tears.

"You're not asleep are you?"

I slowly revealed my red eyes. "No," I replied, almost choking as the tears surged forward.

"Oh, my little poppet, don't cry." She pushed my hair away from my forehead and wiped the tears away from my cheeks. "What's wrong?" she asked with great concern.

"I don't know," I whispered.

"Oh poppet," she said once more, still softly stroking my face.

She put my head rest down and helped me to sit up whilst she puffed my pillows, then took such care over making sure I was comfortable and tucking me in. The tears began to dry up. I felt a lot better for that cry, her gentle motherly approach had calmed my heart and soothed me. She pushed my hair away from my face once more and bent down to kiss me goodnight.

"Sleep well," she whispered, and moved on to the next bed.

I felt so peaceful, I just closed my eyes and fell asleep.

I woke up to a fantastic surprise, to hear from the physician that I could go home in just over a week's time. I could hardly believe my ears; it was marvellous news. Naturally, there had to be an "if" to follow – "if I could maintain my weight". I did not have to put on more weight, just maintain my present weight. I had not reached my target weight, but the summer holidays were coming up and the doctors decided to let me home on a trial basis as my mother would be there during the day.

Did those days till the end of my being in hospital drag on! It was like the last few feet of climbing Mount Everest; each day seemed longer and longer and I certainly was not without my difficulties either. I wondered when it would all end, but I realised that it was important at this stage to look back and compare it with the earlier times, recognising the trials I had been through and managed to overcome.

At the start of the following week the doctors came

round and confirmed that I could go home on Friday. I really felt they meant it this time. My weight had not fallen for several days and they were obviously pleased that I had managed to maintain it; they recognised stability in my illness. For once the sun was shining in my life, and I could not wait to tell my parents the news that my coming home was definite. During visiting hours we sat and talked about the things we would do together when I had left hospital.

I was, however, a little worried about going home and how I would cope, as I knew that I was nowhere near cured of anorexia. Whether I was in hospital or at home, I still faced the same problem – that I was anorexic. Although I knew that at home I would have the support of my parents, I was also aware that I would no longer have the security that I was used to in hospital. As well as facing the difficulties over eating, I would have to cope with the pressures from a hostile world. Even so, I was looking forward to leaving hospital and being in a more natural environment. I had seen so many people come and go, I could not believe that at last I was the one going.

The night before I was due to leave I just could not sleep. My toes kept on twitching with excitement and my mind was bubbling away. I was woken up at 6.00 a.m.

"Who's going home today then?"

It was the voice of the same auxiliary nurse who had been so kind the evening that I was feeling depressed. I turned over, opened my eyes and smiled.

"I can't believe it," I said.

That morning was the longest I had ever experienced; anticipation I suppose. After breakfast the paper boy came on the rounds with his trolley. I always knew it was him with his outbursts of whistles, songs and corny jokes. He was enough to give you inspiration on a dreary morning. He had not had a lot of custom from me but he always passed a joke in my direction. When Helen had been in the next bed, he would start singing or chatting about the two terrible Helens – double trouble!

I had my curtains still drawn round me but I could hear his cheery voice and squeaking wheels coming in my direction. I wanted to say goodbye to him, but there was no hope, I was shut in. I could see the outline of the trolley outside my curtains, then I heard, "First there was double trouble, then trouble, and now there'll be no trouble!"

I knew he was referring to the fact that I was going today. "That's right," I added.

"Bye then, Helen number two," he said in a raised humorous voice.

"Bye," I replied.

The medicine trolley came round. I thought perhaps I would be relieved of any drugs seeing that I was going home, but obviously that was just wishful thinking. The sun streamed in through the window and beat on my back. I lay and imagined myself on a warm, sandy beach, surrounded by tropical plants, the gentle swishing of the waves lulling me to sleep – then Concorde flew over and ruined my fantasy world. After lunch I sat and waited patiently.

"Hello. I've come to check your belongings."

One of the student nurses handed me a black plastic bag, helped me to put everything that I had with me into it, then drew the curtains round and told me to get dressed. I changed into the towelling tracksuit which I had used for physiotherapy and sat on the edge of my bed. Then I heard the scales being pushed in my direction.

"You don't want to weigh me, do you?" I asked the sister with foreboding.

"Afraid so," she replied with a smile.

"Can I sit on the scales like this or do I have to change into the usual clothes?"

"You'll have to change I'm afraid love, otherwise it will give an incorrect reading."

So once again I changed, only to have to re-dress afterwards. I watched expectantly whilst she marked my new weight on the graph. "Help!" I gasped to myself, "I've gone down, that means I won't be going home today." Luckily, however, it did not affect my being able to leave. Minor changes in weight are bound to occur due to water balance.

Shortly afterwards my mother arrived. I saw her talking to the sister; she was presenting the basket of fruit which she had bought as a thank you to all the nurses.

I said all my goodbyes to the other patients that I knew and then to the nurses. The porter wheeled me to the nurses' station and down towards the door of the ward.

"Don't come back will you, Helena." Sister called after me with a sense of humour.

"I'll come to see you but not stay."

So off I went, six stone, two pounds, and a long road to recovery.

Pretence

Pretend you're happy when you're blue
It isn't very hard to do,
Close your eyes and you'll be there
To find a world that'll really care.

The blazing earth will no longer burn
And fear never return,
The darkening shadow shall flee
Setting your heart free.

The glimmering landscape comes into sight
But to keep the sun is no longer a fight,
There is no rugged path in life
Along which you struggle and strive.

No more is there an ocean bare
Love and happiness ride there,
And people stand with their arms wide
Warmly to welcome you inside.

The birds' songs were melodious, the smell of the flowers sweet, the sky blue and the sun felt warm on my face as I was wheeled from the overpowering smell of medication out into the fresh air. I stood up and took a deep breath, inhaling the pureness of the air. How exhilarated I felt to face the summer in all its glory. There certainly was no melancholy in that short-lived moment of my life. The strangest thing was having left the memories of spring behind when I was taken into hospital, and stepping out to see the summer in its prime, as though the past three months had been totally non-existent.

As I climbed into the car ready to be taken home, I could feel the radiance from my mother's face. It must have been a wonderful time for her too, after having driven away from her frequent visits with a lonely, empty feeling. This time that empty space was filled and she was taking me home for good. However kind everyone had been and however much I had become a part of Adelaide ward, it was a relief to be leaving it behind. We turned into a wide road, each side lined by shady trees, and headed for the town centre. The world seemed so busy, as though it had been speeded up, cars zooming past and people dashing from shop to shop. It was exhausting to watch.

It was mid-afternoon by the time we arrived home. Immediately I was greeted by my cat who rapturously rubbed against my legs, purring with content. I felt as though I was in another world; it was strange to see so much activity and life. I felt a new appreciation and sensitivity towards the world; everything was so beautiful – the luscious green trees, the multi-coloured flowers, the smell of new-mown grass and the way in which the sun blazed from a brilliant blue sky. There was so much colour and beauty all around. It was such a lovely day that it seemed a shame not to be out in the open and enjoying it, so after I had had a drink my mother put a sunbed in the garden and I sat down on it, half shaded by the crab-apple tree.

No sooner had I sat down than the doorbell went. My mother answered it, and came over to me carrying a beautiful bouquet of flowers; they were from my Salvation Army friend, B.E. Then a friend came over with some sweet peas from her garden, and another came round with a welcome home card and some notelets.

I had been sitting outside for about fifteen minutes when my face began to itch furiously, and then my legs and arms began to itch. It became so intense that I was forced to retreat inside. The same thing happened the following day. I was sitting in the shade, but after no more than ten minutes my skin began to itch and then burn terribly; I could not bear to be outside any longer. I did not understand why this was happening as I had never been allergic to the sun before. Later I learned that it was one of the many side effects of the drug that I had been on – largactil.

For the first few weeks after leaving hospital I slept downstairs, as I was still very weak. My muscles had wasted away having not had any exercise, or even physiotherapy, for a couple of months. This meant that day to day activities, including walking, were both tiring and painful. I found that I was waking up very early in the morning and by mid-afternoon was extremely tired, so I usually slept for a couple of hours after lunch. To begin with I was still eating very little indeed and my weight, rather than increasing, fell to barely six stone again. My mother feared that I would lose even more and said that whatever happened I must try to keep my weight above six stone. I found eating very difficult. It was a battle of wills, but was helped by my mother taking me out to pub lunches. We nearly always had mixed salads and meat as I found that raw foods, unlike cooked foods, did not nauseate me and the variety of salads and the good presentation made the meal far more appetising.

My parents were very supportive during this time. They were aware of both my physical pain amd mental turmoil, and did all that they could to help me. Besides my mother taking me out to pub lunches, we would visit new places, spend the day in scenic areas and go for picnics by the river. My sister and I were getting on a lot better, and when she came home at weekends we would quite often do things together as a family. It was lovely to feel united as a family and to be able to talk to Ruth about ordinary, everyday things without feelings of bitterness and jealousy between us. When I was in hospital she was super with the get-well cards she sent me and we began to see each other more as individuals rather than enemies.

As good as my family were to me, however, I could not help feeling disheartened over the life that I was leading. I watched other girls of sixteen start new jobs, plan their A-level syllabus, drive around on mopeds and socialise in the evenings. They led happy, independent lives and there was I sitting at home struggling to regain normal health, watching my young life, supposedly the happiest days of my life, slip away before my very eyes. Compared with the average teenager I was living in a solitary, unhappy world.

As the weeks went past, the feeling of having to "make it to the top" pressed upon me heavily. I sat back and thought about my solitary world and the unrealistic life that I was leading. My life benefited no one, and particularly not myself. Ever since I had left hospital I had wasted valuable time and achieved nothing worthwhile. I thought to myself, "I should be getting on with living, not sitting around waiting." I am the sort of person who has to be busy doing something, to feel that I am worthwhile. For me life has to have a meaning and an objective. If I do not have a sense of achievement, as I did not at that time, then life is a waste of time. I became restless and knew that I had to find something to do: I succeeded in getting a part-time job as a breakfast waitress. The hotel was only two

minutes' walk from my house, and the work involved just a
couple of hours early in the morning. The job was ideal: it
gave me the independence and personal contact that I
needed, without being tiring, as well as giving me a sense
of achievement.

I was beginning to organise my life and feel in
command again. I had acquired a keen interest in cooking
and spent a lot of time preparing foods that I personally
did not like, such as cakes, taking great care and precision
over the decoration. I enjoyed making and decorating
cakes, but considered them to be a piece of artwork, to be
viewed by all and eaten by anyone except myself. I had not
put on much weight, but was happy like that; I neither felt
fat nor thin and was managing to eat just enough to keep
me going. I was even enjoying some foods although I had
no appetite or, I should say, hunger. I think it is important
to notice the difference between appetite and hunger. I
consider appetite to be something that the mind desires
and hunger to be something that the stomach desires.
When someone has an appetite then they fancy food
because it is to their liking; if on the other hand someone
has no appetite then they feel nauseated by food. When
someone is hungry then their bodies crave food because
their gastric juices are churning and their glycogen
supplies are in need of replenishment; if someone is not
hungry then they have no hunger pains.

I was thankful that the child psychiatrist had not
managed to admit me into the psychiatric hospital as she
had wanted to. I would still have been in hospital,
surrounded by sick and mentally disturbed people, my
whole life centred around my weight, diet and emotional
conflicts. It would have been months before I could have
left. The thought of still being in hospital was unbearable.
At least being at home I had the moral support of my
parents and I could get on with living, and not have to
worry about reaching a target weight. Yet at times I wished
that I was in hospital, receiving medical help and support
outside the family. Really I did not know what I wanted; I
was confused.

A month after I had started my part-time job I decided that I needed to think about my future career. I could not bear the thought of working for only two hours a day and not training for a career. My ideas of taking spanish, food and nutrition, and art A-levels at a near-by convent school followed by a BA in graphic design, had fallen through; the thought of school was too much. So, I had to think again. Besides art, I had been keen on food and nutrition O-level. My thoughts about taking a catering course were confirmed when we received a telephone call from my headmistress.

"I've got your two latest O-level results, Helena. Are you ready?"

"Yes," I replied with anticipation and excitement.

"History first, B for Betty, then food and nutrition, A for Aunty. Have you got that? Aunty Betty!"

I was really pleased and straight away I started to look through college prospectuses for suitable courses. I decided to apply for the general catering course which would give me City and Guilds qualifications. My application was seven months too late, but nevertheless I was called up for an interview.

The day that the interview was taking place, I had an appointment to see the consultant physician at the hospital. He was very pleased with the progress I had made. I had managed to put on some weight and at six stone six pounds, I was only one pound under the weight he had set for me to reach before leaving hospital. He was pleased that I was going along for an interview at the technical college and wished me good luck, and made another appointment for me to see him. As I went from the hospital to the college I thought one thing, "Thank goodness I am taking a step towards my career, not a hospital bed!"

When I arrived at the college, I had a very informal interview with the head of the department of food, health and fashion. He advised me to take an Ordinary National Diploma in hotel and catering operations and offered me a place on the course to commence in two weeks. I owe many thanks to the head of department for accepting me whilst I was still very ill and could have been a liability.

I really had an incentive to get better. I knew that if I wanted to get the diploma then I had to keep well enough to carry out the two years' work. I could not let myself, my family or the college down by having to go back into hospital. I felt exhilarated that I had done something positive and that the prospects for the future were looking quite good. I did not have much time to worry about whether I would cope with life at college because there was such a lot to distract my attention. There was my equipment and clothing to buy, visits to the local education authority and many other things.

The day before the enrolment I became very apprehensive. I was not sure how easy it would be to make friends and what people would think of my appearance. I wondered how I would be able to stand up to the day to day activities, walking, climbing the never-ending stairs and writing at fast speeds. I worried about not being able to see notes on the blackboard and getting behind in my work. Most of all I worried about how I could cope with lunch-times. Teenagers wolfing down packets of crisps, cans of coke and bars of chocolate. At some point I would no doubt be compelled to join in with these crazy habits. The thought was daunting.

When the enrolment day came I was amazed by the relaxed atmosphere of the college, the freedom and the respect which the tutors had for their students as individuals. They were always making jokes and enabled one to feel on the same level as themselves; we were not constantly spoken down to. It was quite different from what I had been used to at school and I knew that if I tried hard I could enjoy myself. By the end of the first day my conviction that I was going to be happy had grown. I had really enjoyed the lectures and I had made friends with one of the girls on the course. We remained friends for the two years. I was, however, extremely tired by the end of the day. Going to lectures and doing some written work in the evening was as much as I could manage for the whole of the first term. All my energies were directed towards my work and I very rarely socialised. I was happy putting all my time and energy into the course, because I derived great satisfaction from being conscientious, which I did not derive from socialising with people my own age. I could not laugh like other people; it was too much effort. I thought that other people would think me strange because of my appearance and apparent solemnity and I was hypersensitive to criticism.

As the weeks progressed and I became accustomed to college life and the various subjects which the course involved, my self-confidence grew a little. I was not without my difficulties, and there was one time in particular when I felt like giving up the course. Physically it was too much effort. I could not join in with the gaiety of the other students; I felt distant and alone. I lived in fear of being a failure and of criticism over my work, appearance and eating habits. I dreaded the day that we would have a test and I would not be able to read the questions on the board, the time that I could not stand up to a day's work in the kitchen and I would collapse. I had been living in a world of pretence, dreaming of being on a beautiful island, covered by brilliant white sand and sparkling sea. Miles of empty space to run and feel free. Then I would be forced to return to reality. When I saw the life that I was leading my dreams faded. My island of paradise changed into dark woods in which I was trapped and had no room to breathe.

Despite the knowledge that there was something wrong, the tutors did not treat me any differently from the other students which gave me the determination to carry on as if all was well. I felt that they respected me as an individual and that even if I did not, they had confidence in my work and in me. This was particularly evident with the food science tutor, to whom I owe many thanks.

One of the hardest things to cope with was the production kitchen. As well as the energy to be on my feet for half the day and cook for large numbers, I had to cope with the vast quantity of food, the smell whirling around me. I remember the first time that I was cooking for the training restaurant; I was meat chef. Ten pounds of beef was slapped in front of me; I stuck the knife in to cut it up, blood and meat juice oozed out, the odour wafted up; there was a layer of fat, horrible fat, and I was overcome by a profound feeling of nausea. As I cut through the mound of meat, my arm ached, I felt that I would never last out until the end of the morning. I did. As I was leaving the room at the end of the lesson, the tutor grabbed my arm, "You need to put some weight on," she told me. I knew that only too well but could not do anything about it.

She was well aware that besides lacking physical strength, I lacked self-confidence, but also knew that if I wanted to go into catering as a career then I had to overcome both of these. There was nothing that she could do to help me overcome my physical weakness other than to warn me that I could never cope unless I put on weight, but she could help me to gain confidence. Her way of doing this was to push me to the extreme and face me with tasks that I did not believe I could carry out, thereby proving to myself that I was as capable as anyone else. At the time it did not seem to be the kindest thing to do, but it certainly made me fight and hardened me, as well as giving me the determination to succeed.

At the end of my first term at college I had another appointment with the consultant physician at the hospital. I walked rather nervously into out-patients. I knew that I had not put on any weight and I feared what he would do. I sat down until the sister came over to me. "Let's check your weight, Helena," she said.

My stomach turned over as I heard the squeak of the scales being wheeled towards me. Slowly, I sat down; she checked the reading, and scribbled down some figures. Then the consultant called me into his room. He looked at the notes and piece of paper which the sister had handed to him. His eyes stared straight through me, and with the house doctor also present, looking sternly at me, I felt extremely uncomfortable. Seeing the two of them standing there suddenly brought back all the memories of hospital. I remembered how I dreaded the doctor's rounds on the ward. The horrid feeling of lying in bed surrounded by white coats and staring faces, firing questions. I felt sick with fear. The feeling gradually died away as the consultant asked me how I felt and what I was doing. He was pleased that I had managed to maintain my weight and that I had been accepted at college. He decided that I was better off away from doctors and hospitals and that there was no need for me to make another appointment with him, unless at any stage my parents or I were worried. It certainly was a good start to the Christmas holidays; I was free, no longer tied to a hospital.

The following term I had something wonderful to look forward to which helped me to get through the term with few worries. I was going to Bermuda to stay with my cousin, Kathie, during the Easter holidays. It was something to look forward to, an incentive to keep well and a topic to talk about in the spoken english lecture!

The term began with me catching some kind of bug. (Colds and flu were something that I had very rarely had since getting anorexia.) It was not bad enough to take time off college, but left me feeling tired, dizzy and heavy-headed.

I was one of the students from the catering department taking part in the Bournemouth Food and Wine Exhibition, an exhibition and competition open to students and professional caterers. I had decided to enter the fruit cake class, and a lot of time and effort was spent on the preparation for the exhibition. Besides being very keen on practical cookery, I took a special interest in hygiene and microbiology, and food science, which included nutrition. I found them fascinating.

At this stage, however, my anorexia developed into more than purely a physical illness; it became an obsession as well. I weighed myself twice a day to see whether I had put on even one pound. This was not because I was trying to lose weight but because the weight-phobia aspect of anorexia nervosa had taken hold of me very tightly. I lived in absolute fear of reaching seven stone. When I stood on the scales and they read six stone nine pounds, I panicked; I was only five pounds less than the dreaded seven stone mark.

I then looked in the mirror and the figure that stared back at me, rather than the scrawny being which others saw, was fat and ugly. This phenomenon of the mirror-image was not peculiar to me but a common factor in anorexia nervosa. One actually sees a distorted picture of one's body. Seeing my body looking fat and lumpy at six stone nine pounds reinforced my terror at the thought of reaching seven stone, let alone the normal eight or nine stone, the usual weight for women of my height.

My eating habits were even more bizarre than my conception of weight. When I first went to college I used to go into the refectory for lunch, which usually consisted of a bowl of soup or salad; very occasionally, if I was feeling enterprising I would have chicken pie, carefully putting aside the pastry of course. Later I started to take sandwiches to college. The thought of two slices of bread, spread with fat and filled with protein was too much. Either I ate the meat and disposed of the bread or else disposed of the lot in the nearest bin. I carried out this practice for nearly two years before my parents noticed. I was so cunning and deceitful over hiding food that I do not think any of my college friends had a clue what was going on. In the evening I always ate with my family, but was very fussy over what I ate. I enjoyed planning and cooking meals, but always gave myself a very small helping; then afterwards I would go and pick at the left-overs or at food in the fridge. Where possible I avoided eating meals and food in general.

Gradually, I began to put on some weight. I felt terrible. I was depressed at my lack of self-control; I picked at food non-stop but still could not bring myself to eat a full meal.

The extra pounds that I had gained made me feel extremely uncomfortable; when I sat down I felt as though there were ripples of fat around my waist. My clothes felt tighter, as though they were gripping my body, even if they were loose. I had reached seven stone. Two of the girls on my course commented that I had put on weight and how much better I looked. Contrary to what one would expect, their comment made me feel even worse. The thought that other people could notice a change must mean that I had put on a lot of weight. I must look terrible, I must be fat, I thought. The fact was that I could not accept that I looked different. Then, during the last week of term I caught another flu-bug. I had four days off college, during which time I lost a couple of pounds; my weight was now six stone twelve pounds.

The day after I broke up for the Easter holidays, I flew to Bermuda. My cousin was waiting at the airport to meet me. We had not seen each other for six years and I feared that she might not recognise me, but she did. Also there to greet me was the Canon of Bermuda Cathedral, Peter, and his wife Joy. Kathie had been staying with them since she had had to leave her apartment. We drove to the city of Hamilton where they lived. I looked out of the window at the brilliant turquoise sea, the multi-coloured flowers, the palm trees and pastel-coloured houses with their white roofs. I could not believe that I was actually on the fairytale island to which so often I had dreamt of running away when I was depressed.

For the two weeks that I was in Bermuda I was really happy, a happiness I had not known before. As the holiday progressed I found myself changing so that when I returned I had gained a measure of self-confidence and could laugh again, whereas earlier in the illness it was an effort even to smile.

The first thing to confront me on my return was the college examination in which, to my surprise, I did well. In general I began to take more interest in life. I did not feel so divorced from people, began to mix more easily and occasionally socialise in the evenings which I am sure was in part due to my experiences in Bermuda where, with Peter's witty jokes, we rarely stopped laughing. He was hysterically funny and cunning and the only time I managed to catch him out was with the camera.

As I became able to mix more easily with the other members of my course and take more interest in the life around me, others seemed to notice that I was there. I felt my personality, which had appeared flat and non-existent, developing. I began to feel that I was a person in my own right. People then started to ask me about my experience with anorexia and I was able to talk about it and face it squarely which I had not previously been able to do.

To my delight and amazement menstruation had started again towards the end of my holiday. Usually this takes place only when a fair body weight has been maintained for some time. I was only just over seven stone and had to go through puberty for a second time with all the associated changes and traumas. Perhaps this accounts for some of the difficulties which were yet to come in spite of my new found confidence.

In Bermuda, in the relaxed atmosphere, even my feelings towards food had changed. I no longer suffered from nausea and although I was never very hungry I had an appetite. The continuous festivity, going out to meals with food beautifully cooked and presented, and the frequent barbecues with all the fun and effort needed, had made eating a pleasure. This, I am sure, helped me in the summer term when I went out on work experience with two other girls from my course to a small wine bar in my home town. We got on very well with the owners and people working there. Sometimes we worked during the day and sometimes in the evening, both cooking and serving. It was good experience and great fun.

The main problem was that I found I was putting on weight much faster than I would have liked and panicked at the thought of never being able to stop putting it on. I looked at my new body image with disgust. I was seven and a half stone and felt extremely uncomfortable. Whenever I tried new clothes on they did not fit. The clothes I had were tight and I felt that when I leant over rolls of fat were hanging over the top of my jeans; they clung to my legs which were no longer straight like sticks but bulged out at the top – horrible, horrible sight, I thought. The trouble was that I could not accept my developing body; I could not cope alone. My mind and body were not compatible.

For the following six weeks I worked as a commis chef at a hotel in Bournemouth. It successfully put me off wanting to go into catering as a career! But it was very good experience and proved beneficial in my second year at college. It was extremely hard work, the hours were long and unsociable and the constant handling of food hard to cope with. Being concerned with food all day and quite often having to face the less pleasant tasks of having to mop up meat juice that had turned sour with the heat releasing the most appalling odour, nauseated me. The last thing I wanted to do was eat. I think that if it had not been for the support of the people with whom I was staying I could easily have lost weight. When I finished work at Bournemouth, I went youth hostelling in France with my boyfriend, Andy, with whom I had resumed a good friendship some months after coming out of hospital. We had a lovely time travelling right from the north to the south coast. The freedom and independence really helped me.

I returned to college for my final year a far more healthy and confident person. I sensed that people's reactions towards me were completely different from what they had been previously. I was no longer stared at, I was brought into conversations, people asked my opinion about topics rather than ignoring me. I felt more like one of the others. I enjoyed the second year even more than the first year. My main aim was to be conscientious and to use my capabilities to the full. I ensured that I remained near the top of the class in all subjects, to satisfy myself if no one else.

Maintaining a high standard of work was not difficult. The only thing that was a major problem was having to struggle with the psychological aspect of anorexia nervosa which had run away with me and was destined to disrupt my life. I lived in hatred of my woman-shaped body, because no one had helped me to accept it.

The last time I had weighed myself I had been seven and a half stone; I dreaded putting on more weight and feared that I would never be able to stop gaining weight. Consequently I refused to weigh myself; I could not face reality. I still disposed of my sandwiches at college and quite often spent part of the afternoon feeling faint, dizzy or with a bad headache because I had not eaten. When I was alone I had bursts of uncontrollable eating which left me feeling bloated, guilty and shocked at what had happened. I hated myself because I had no self-discipline, no self-respect. I felt stuffed and unclean, dirty and savage.

To relieve me of these feelings and to cleanse my body, in desperation I took to purging. A miserable, degrading and self-destructing thing to do. It was probably because of this that at times I experienced a terrible pain in my bones, especially those in my legs; my body was obviously depleted of calcium. My weight remained steady but my abnormal attitude towards food and my body haunted me. This adversely affected relationships. I was very sensitive to other people's remarks about my eating habits or weight. I was very touchy, even short-tempered with my parents, in particular my father to whom I was rather cold and always on the defensive. If I was offered food other than at mealtimes I regarded it as a subtle way of wanting to fatten me up. I was experiencing mental torture – something that I would never wish to go through again.

I kept in touch with one of the nurses who had been working on Adelaide ward for most of the time that I was in hospital. She understood anorexia nervosa very well.

She once said:

It is so easy to bluff your way through life kidding everyone that things are fine – unfortunately you can't fool yourself. The main thing to realise is that there is no miracle cure: it can take years for you to recover fully and enjoy food again so a great deal of perseverance and considerable support will help you. There are so many people who don't understand anorexia, I think it would be helpful if you went to a doctor who is realistic and does not fob you off. He will keep you on an even keel, and if you find yourself losing weight you will feel yourself letting him down. Don't feel you are alone, crazy or abnormal; don't expect a miracle; just don't give up.

Her advice and support were very helpful.

12

Sometimes I feel so insecure

My eyes sink back
Into deep, dark holes
As a stream of tears
Trickles down my saddened face.

A sharp pain shoots
Through my lifeless body
Ripping my heart
And piercing my head.

I clench my jaw
To lock the tears
And stare into space,
My eyes a translucent glaze.

My grip gives way
To an outburst of water
Flooding my childlike body;
Sometimes I feel so insecure.

Bournemouth had provided useful experience not only for my OND course but also of life – some good and some unpleasant. Nearly being raped by the second chef and the heat and hard work in the hotel kitchens in a hot summer contrasted with the very great kindness of the two church families who had me to stay between them during those weeks. I began to see how life out in the world has its dark and light sides equally as much as in hospital or school. It was there that I came across an article about anorexia nervosa and SARA (The Society for the Advancement of Research into Anorexia). With my maturing attitude to life I was beginning to look outwards and have a greater desire both to do more research into this mystifying disease and help others. I therefore sent a donation and became a member. The leaflet quoted below spoke clearly to me although at that time I did not realise what far reaching effects it would have upon my life.

Anorexia Nervosa can and does kill. Do you know:
    Anorexia is a disease of mind and body. It is an eating disorder often accompanied by profound fear of normal weight. Severe wasting and loss of periods are character-istic.
    It is far too common. A specialist has estimated that one in two hundred young women suffers from it. About one in ten anorexics is male. This incidence is comparable with that of diabetes. Older people suffer from it too.
    Sufferers can't just "snap out of it". An average case can take five years. Many never fully recover.
    No one knows how it starts or why a patient recovers. Yet little balanced research is being done.
    Successful specialist treatment is seldom available. SARA hopes to save.

The Society for the Advancement of Research into Anorexia is a registered charity committed:

To promote thorough research into this disease, to discover its causes, to find the best forms of treatment and to establish means of early diagnosis. Thus years of distress can be prevented.

To instigate more and better facilities for specialist treatment, including sustained follow-up care.

To encourage general understanding and awareness of anorexia, so to reduce the extended suffering of patients and their families.

In February I decided that the one thing I wanted to do was to prevent other people suffering in the way in which I had. Even if I was not completely over anorexia, I could not bear to see other young girls go through the same agony. I wrote to one of the secretaries and prime mover behind SARA to find out about setting up a local branch. She agreed to my establishing the first branch and told me what this involved. On May 1st 1982, Berkshire SARA was launched at a buffet supper attended by medics, heads of schools and the general public. Part of the press coverage read:

> Now at eighteen years old Helena can look at anorexia objectively and say that she is better, if not cured. Now with the pain and anguish of starving to death at least partially behind her, her main aim is to help other sufferers and hopefully prevent more people from falling victim to the disease.
>
> The new branch was launched this month in Reading when Clare Jones, one of the original members of SARA, came to Berkshire to help Helena to explain to people the facts about anorexia.

I was pleased that I had done something positive and that I had something definite to work for – raising funds for research to take place. To me, equally important to raising money, was to enlighten the general public about the complexities of anorexia nervosa, or as Nicola Gannon, a newspaper reporter and good friend, once said, "To bring anorexia out of the cupboard and on the stage."

More and more I realised how little the general public understood the illness and how little sympathy it gained. Too often it is thought of as self-imposed and concerned only with dieting teenagers who ought to snap out of it and pull themselves together, when really it is a callous disease which destroys the sufferer and the morale of her family. Knowing that so many people's view of anorexia was distorted and the degree of impatience that it elicits, saddened and even angered me. My determination to prove otherwise became so strong that my self-confidence increased and when asked I was able to talk about anorexia nervosa to the public, to the press and on the radio. It was at that stage that I decided to write this book. When I was in hospital I kept an illustrated diary which the nurses and patients loved to read. Several of the nurses said I should have it published. I did not give it a second thought until this time, when I decided that I wanted to write a little more than just my hospital diary, so *Puppet on a String* evolved. I felt compelled to write it down on paper to get it off my mind – out of sight, out of mind.

A book of this type is not the place in which one can go in depth into the many theories of the causes of anorexia. It seems to me that within the medical profession there is considerable confusion and often difficulty, not only in deciding on the cause and therefore what treatment to administer, but also in diagnosing the disease in its early stages.

Theories abound in the popular press, some of which relate anorexia to the effect of an unmourned death, childhood traumas, fear of growing up, and the very common idea that slimming has got out of hand. Food allergy, too, has been suggested as a cause for it is well known that the food for which we really crave is the one which does harm. In the later stages of my illness there were some foods which, if I ate them at all, I found difficulty in stopping eating. On looking back it was these foods that I first eliminated from my diet in the early stages of my illness.

The theory which makes sense to me is one suggesting a link between hormones and stress. Dr Connolly, at a SARA symposium in London, spoke of the need to see if hormonal systems could be permanently disturbed by stresses of different types. He also pointed out that many new brain hormones have been discovered which, even in exceedingly low quantities, cause profound behavioural changes. Many of these hormones are concerned with our self-regulating functions such as breathing and eating.

An area in which there seems to be a need for research is in connection with the small gland at the base of the skull known as the hypothalamus, which regulates the pituitary gland. The hypothalamus numbers amongst its other functions the control of thirst, appetite, sexual function and body temperature. There seems to be a strong correlation between this gland and anorexia nervosa, the main features of which are loss of appetite, aversion to food, loss of menstruation and a general lack of interest in sex, along with poor circulation and cold skin. The pineal gland is also linked with the hypothalamus and controls our circadian rhythms which in turn control functions dependent on time, such as sleeping and eating. Not only as a baby was my sleeping rhythm disturbed, but when I had anorexia I rarely had a good night's sleep.

I have already expressed a number of my views over the causes, but to summarise the information very briefly, this is what I consider happens. An individual is put under *pressure*. Whether this is from unresolved emotional conflicts, pressure to lose weight, emphasis on success and high standards of achievement, or whether it is sexual pressure leading to an aversion to growing up, this puts the individual under *stress*. Stress in itself can lead to hormonal changes which result in a lack of appetite and weight loss. It is possible that the hormonal changes take place as a result of a significant weight loss. Whichever way round this is, it still leads to the *illness*, anorexia nervosa. Being a psychosomatic illness it is very much a matter of mind and body. I feel that not until the psychological side is cleared will the physical symptoms disappear, because whilst the pressure is still there the cycle is triggered off.

As well as putting time into SARA I also had to put a lot of energy into college work. Every day the subjects became more intense and my finals crept closer. I did not know what I wanted to do when the course ended. I decided not to worry about what the future held but to concentrate on doing well in my finals. When I started revision for the exams I found myself becoming very tense and my tendency to resort to a number of subterfuges as regards eating became worse. Also I had pain in my shoulder. I felt that I could not cope with the exams alone. If I had tried to I would doubtless have gone back in my tracks. My mother took me to an acupuncturist who helped relieve the pain in my shoulder and gave me a short amount of treatment for anorexia and tension. The treatment worked very well; it enabled me fully to relax and take my finals calmly and confidently.

A week after college ended – I was sad to leave – I started a job at St George's House in Windsor Castle, of which my godfather is the warden. I was filling in for one of the cooks for a month. It was a fantastic experience and a good reference to have but very exhausting and did not help my fight against anorexia. I shared a flat with the other cook, in the castle grounds. We started work at 7.20 a.m., making bread, then sat down for something to eat before preparing breakfast and lunch for the thirty-odd conference guests. This usually took us to about 1.00 p.m., when there was a mad rush to have all the food dished up and in the hot plate or oven and to clear away and wash the equipment. If I had wanted to I could have sat down to a meal at lunch-time, but after dealing with food all morning I could not face eating it so I very rarely ate lunch. Between 2.00 p.m.

and 4.00 p.m. we were off duty. More often than not I sat outside in the sun to take the weight off my feet. The afternoons and evenings were always hectic, running around getting everything ready in time for dinner and doing as much preparation for the next day as possible. By the time work ended at about 8.00 p.m. I was too tired to want to eat; I was not hungry, but sometimes made myself have a meal because I knew what would happen if I did not.

In the evenings I used either to read, write or listen to music, or go out to the pub or fair with some of the domestic assistants and nannies. We had great fun. I felt even more exhilarated when coming back to the castle in the early hours of the morning, approaching the huge overpowering doors and showing identification to the policeman. We would hear the clunk of the bolt and then walk in. The huge stone walls on either side were lit up by lamps and shone a mysterious gold, warm and welcoming but at the same time uncanny. As we walked, one of the guards marched up and down, obviously keeping a watchful eye on us. We passed under an archway which led into the Horseshoe Cloisters, past the entrance to St George's Chapel, with the grand steps gracefully leading up to the ornate door on to which a golden light was thrown and through another archway which led to St George's House. It sounds all so exciting, but we often paid a price for our fun – only four hours sleep before a heavy day's work.

After about two weeks I found myself attacked by the same feelings of despair and depression with which I had so often struggled at school, feelings which I had not experienced since I came out of hospital. I had been unhappy at times, but not come up against this intense sense of loneliness and desperation. As I had done before, I began questioning every aspect of life. When I was alone I cried quietly; once more I stared into the mirror and saw a miserable face, dejected and full of pain. I could not understand why there was such agony behind those tear-stricken eyes – my eyes. On the occasions that my mother came over to see me, she was convinced that I was losing weight and looking unwell and for this reason visited me far more than she would otherwise have done. The last three days brought the end of season cleaning up. We worked through the whole day for several days in succession, and by the end I was worn out.

13

Fading love

Love was once so tender and pure,
A silk lining which clothed my body
And made me feel secure.

The lining has now been torn,
My body, vulnerable to the world
And the sadness that is born.

Pain and bitterness enter in,
Shooting through with a jagged edge
And ripping me apart within.

All warmth has vanished away,
Wind gathers speed, blows over me
And coolness comes to stay.

Love and pain are intertwined,
But one day I hope that love
Without pain I will find.

The end of the summer brought with it an intense emotional experience, with love and pain intertwined, which had a dramatic effect on me and changed my whole perception of life.

As a last minute decision I had agreed to join one of my ex-schoolfriends to do a week's voluntary work as a cook at the CYFA (Christian Youth Fellowship Association) camp in Limpsfield, Surrey.

We arrived at the large old building situated in an expanse of land. As we walked across the driveway towards the front door the sky hung dark over our heads; there was a bite to the air and it was raining. As we entered the building and went up the stairs to our dormitory my mind was filled with too many less favourable memories of school for comfort. Despite the excitement of the work and meetings which lay ahead, I could already feel the sword of pain cutting its way through my body, but I covered up my feelings which I felt were inane.

The following day there was a bustle of activity as the house party arrived, comprised of around one hundred teenagers.

I soon became familiar with the surroundings and accustomed to the routine which put me more at ease. There were about eight cooks and several pantry staff, all of whom worked on a rota system. The system was carefully arranged so that no one missed either the morning or evening meetings. The meetings were a real inspiration and their message became more wonderful each time. We started off by singing several choruses from *Youth Praise* or a similar song book. This was quite often followed by a sketch acted by a few senior members, illustrating an important point or passage in the Bible.

Then there was always a talk given by one of the leaders, with prayers and songs bringing the meeting to a close.

Over the past two years I had become distant from God and even my attending church held no special meaning. I hadn't even taken a Bible to the camp with me, yet each time I walked into the meeting room I felt a yearning in myself for something just out of my reach. I was deeply moved by the songs we sang, and also by the talks and the amazing love – God's love – which radiated from so many people there. I cried tears from my heart to feel the presence of such a wonderful love. An agony flowed through my body as I longed to know this love and for it to fill my heart. Yet I was filled with fear, there was no room for love.

Working in the kitchen during much of the day did not detract from the special moments encountered during the meetings. Whilst preparing the food there was much fellowship; we shared amongst ourselves our reasons for belief in God, what He had done in our lives, what the meeting had meant to us that morning, our problems and difficulties, and far more. During the middle of the morning the pantry staff made coffee and joined the rest of us in the kitchen for a time of prayer and the sharing of a passage from the Bible. If we happened to be hectically busy at that moment then we would make up for the prayer time later, or give our profound apologies to God!

One of the nicest things about working in the kitchen at Limpsfield was the fantastic atmosphere. It was free of the pressures I had experienced elsewhere, and the people cared about each other. There was trust, joy and excitement, rather than constant anxiety. It was nothing unusual to be cooking and singing a chorus at the same time. I remember on one occasion making fruit salad and joining in with a chorus, but each time I went to collect more fruit from the room next door where the boys were peeling potatoes, I came back singing the song they were singing!

One thing I found extremely difficult during this time

was eating. As soon as it was time to eat an intense fear would flood through my body, my stomach would be tied up in knots, I would literally be shaking and could not bring myself to enter the dining room. The noise of a hundred people munching food, the thought of eating three square meals a day and having to face food when I had no appetite, was too much. I think I was at the stage where, given the circumstances, I could have gone right back to square one in anorexia. I had not experienced such a profound fear over eating for a long time and my revulsion towards food, my lack of appetite and hunger and the way in which my stomach tensed up at the thought of eating were exactly the same feelings as those experienced just before I had to go into hospital. Thankfully I was at the right place to halt me in my tracks and I believe there was a definite purpose behind my going through these feelings again, one which God could use for good.

In a moment of desperation I explained my eating difficulties to Sue who, although she did not understand anorexia, was a great help and very nobly spent several mealtimes in the kitchen with me so that I could eat as much or as little as I liked. We often spent the time talking about God, Jesus and the Bible as I tried to grasp the real meaning of faith and its importance.

Another person who helped me a great deal was Paula. She was a really super person who had had her fair share of depression and anxiety. Through having suffered in this way, she understood the mental anguish I was experiencing and we took long walks through the woods discussing the problem. Wandering among the tall, graceful trees and tangled undergrowth, the sun setting in the distance and casting its golden light upon the path, something Paula had emphasised came back to me again and again:

"God wants to set you free, because He loves you as an individual."

The freedom which she spoke of was not just freedom

from anorexia but complete freedom to be oneself. Not to
have that feeling of being tied down and trapped. I could
not fully comprehend such freedom, but I longed for it.
Yet I did not feel that I personally could experience such a
thing. My confusion began to override my aspirations.

Once more people surged into the dining room for
supper. Suddenly, I became panic-stricken and at the same
time nauseated by the smell of the food. In terror, I ran
upstairs. Safe from food I had time to calm down and
gather my thoughts a little. I stood staring out of the
window, supporting my weight on its ledge. The sky was
grey and oppressive, the landscape drab. A sheet of mist
hung in front of the woods and hills, tree-tops faded into
the skyline from which a drizzling rain fell. I had my
notebook at hand and was recalling one of the talks given a
few days previously. One aspect in particular stuck in my
mind, "the closer you get to Jesus, the closer you get to
other people". I tried to illustrate the idea in sketch form; I
paused for a moment. The door opened and Paula walked
in.

"I thought you'd be here," she said. I carried on
sketching and she looked over my shoulder at what I'd
done.

"What you have written is very true," she said warmly.
"You do get closer to other people. But we have to learn to
love ourselves first, because we are told in the command-
ments to love God with all our heart. If our hearts are filled
with hatred of ourselves, we cannot love God fully. Then
we are told to love our neighbour as ourselves. If we hate
ourselves, we hate our neighbour. So before anything else
we have to learn to accept ourselves."

"How can I love myself to the degree which you are
talking about whilst I still have anorexia?" I asked. "It's a
deceitful, secretive disease. I can only feel guilty and hate
myself for the things I do. But at the same time I can't
control it; it's something you can't just snap out of – it's a
disease."

"I know, but God can help you. Remember in

Philippians it says, 'Don't worry about anything, but in all your prayers ask God for what you need' (Phil. 4:6).''

I looked down at the piece of paper on which I had been doodling.

"You probably won't understand this, Paula, but I am scared of getting better."

"I do understand," she replied gently. "You have a lot to be scared of. It can't be an easy problem to overcome, but offer it to God and you will no longer be frightened. He loves you. 'There is no fear in love; perfect love drives out all fear' (1 John 4:18). Shall we go somewhere quiet and pray?"

"Yes," I replied.

"God loves you Helena," Paula had said. The more I thought about those few words, the more wonderful they seemed to be. Realising that, "We love because God first loved us" (1 John 4:19) made things even clearer. Because God loves us, we are able to love ourselves.

Everything appeared to be linking up now. The missing piece to the puzzle had been found and I was now able to see the connection.

> GOD loves YOU
> which enables
> YOU to love YOURSELF
> you can then love
> OTHERS as YOURSELF
> and therefore love
> GOD
> with all your heart

Later I was reading the Bible and discovered a passage which summed up everything I was learning about God and love. Love comes from God.

Dear friends, let us love one another, because love comes from God. Whoever loves is a child of God and knows God (1 John 4:7).

The passage continues:

> If this is how God loved us, then we should love one
> another. No one has ever seen God, but if we love one
> another, God lives in union with us, and His love is
> made perfect in us (1 John 4:11–12).

One evening, whilst the house party was gathered in the
old wood-panelled dining room having its late night
dinner, I stood talking to Sue. She was trying to explain
how great God's love is for us and how He longs for us
fully to accept Him into our lives.

"Just remember that God is standing there knocking on
your door; you've only got to invite Him in," she told me.

I spent virtually the whole of that night and the
following day thinking about what Sue had said. I realised
that throughout my life I had been conversing with God
through the letter-box. Not once, when I knew very well
that He was out there, or even when He knocked, had I
opened the door and invited Him in. There was a hidden
reason as to why I always kept the door closed between us:
inside, my house was in a terrible mess, it needed a
thorough clean before I could possibly let Him in. By the
time evening came I had actually grasped the fact that God
doesn't mind how bad the mess inside our house is. It is
His work and pleasure to help us clear up, and through
allowing Him to do so we are changed into better people.

Suddenly my heart overflowed with a never-ending
warmth. I knew, at that moment, that God was knocking
at my door but this time I really wanted to open it wide and
let Him inside. I leapt with joy, and bubbling over with
excitement I rushed to Sue's room to tell her the news.

"That's wonderful, Helena," she said, her eyes shining
with delight. I was so happy I could not stop smiling; nor
could Sue.

"Shall we pray together?" I said.

"Yes," she replied, grasping my hand.

The faith in the few words that she spoke was

tremendous, "Oh Father! Thank You that Helena wants to let You into her heart." I felt a vibration pass through her hands into mine. I wanted God's love to grow and grow in my heart.

"Have you got a Bible?" she asked.

"Not a modern one."

"Right, let's go and get one then! The cooks are allowed a free book, let's go and fetch yours now."

We ran down the stairs, along the corridor and into the library.

Just before I went to sleep that night, I opened my Bible at random. The picture which lay in front of me was the feeding of the five thousand, a parable I knew well, but this time I understood something personal that I'm sure God was telling me. Here were five thousand people who had had food enough to satisfy their hunger and whose hearts were filled with gratitude. I had food enough to satisfy my hunger, far more than they, but I rejected it; there was no gratitude in my heart. I was too concerned with myself.

I glanced at the passage below the picture.

If anyone wants to come with me, he must forget self, take up his cross every day, and follow me. For whoever wants to save his own life will lose it, but whoever loses his life for my sake will save it. Will a person gain anything if he wins the whole world but is himself lost or defeated? Of course not! (Luke 9:23-25).

I think God was teaching me two things through that passage, first humility, and also that His path is the hardest to follow but the only one with treasure worth having at the end.

In the morning I felt excited and overjoyed at my new discoveries about God and changed feelings towards life.

During each of the remaining days Sue and I spent half an hour reading a passage from the Bible and trying to find out its meaning. I was hungry for God's word and gained a great deal from these studies.

I wasn't only hungry for the word, but also for food! Very gradually my appetite was returning, fear was losing its grip and tension was calming down. I was able to enter the dining room to eat a full meal and my stomach even started to have hunger pangs again. It was a wonderful feeling!

One evening I was talking to Nicky, a friend I had made a few days previously. She had a gentle and caring attitude and her eyes shone brilliantly whenever she spoke of God. She had been asking me about anorexia and explaining what happiness I could find in life if only I could get over the disease.

"One thing I really pray for you, Helena, is that you find a really good friend when you go back home."

She had her guitar with her and was quietly strumming a few chords. She suggested that we went somewhere quiet and sang some songs. A group of us, including Paula and my school friend Mary, sat on the step to the chancel and the others on the floor in front. The chapel was dimly lit with a golden light which was warm and welcoming. I felt so content in the beautifully peaceful atmosphere. As we sang quietly to the music of the guitar the room was filled with love. Everyone sang with such meaning and the words of the songs moved me deeply. Suddenly I felt a pain shoot through my body, it was as though I were being torn to shreds. I stared straight ahead, tears rolled down my cheeks. I could see Jesus suffering on the cross; what agony he experienced.

Nicky put her arm round me. "Is there anything you want to sing, Helena?" she whispered.

"Jesus take me as I am; I can come no other way," I replied.

The words moved me deeply. I really wanted Jesus to take me. He died to save me.

When we had finished singing everyone left the chapel except for Nicky, Paula, Carrie and myself.

"Do you really want to know Jesus?" Nicky asked me.

"Yes," I replied. "I love Him." My voice was full of pain.

"Pray then, Helena," Nicky gently urged.

"I can't."

Paula took hold of my hand. "Do you want us to pray for you, Helena?"

"Yes, please."

They all laid their hands on me and prayed.

Two days later the camp drew to a close. My time there had been one of intense pain intertwined with awe and wonder. A time for searching, for new realisations. Above all else, I had discovered the meaning to life. I said goodbye to Limpsfield with the knowledge that there would always be someone with me through both the rough and the smooth. Just as I was leaving Paula gave me a book called *Love Yourself*, about self-acceptance and depression. Sue gave me a passage to look up in the Bible: "So I am sure that God, who began this good work in you, will carry it on until it is finished" (Phil. 1:6).

I had so much to say thank you for. Even more so when my mother came to pick me up. As we set off home I opened my post which she had brought with her. The first letter I opened was my Diploma result – it was a pass. I was pleased that I had attained a Diploma but very disappointed that it was not a distinction. I went on ripping open the envelopes and half-heartedly reading the contents. I had a shock when I read one of the letters.

"Hey Mum! Listen to this," I said in a tone of amazement. "Dear Ms Wilkinson, You have been judged by a distinguished panel of seven experts to be the winner in the student category of the Leverclean Award 1982 – congratulations. The presentation of your £500 prize will..."

"Hang on a second, let me stop the car and have a look at this," my mother interrupted.

I showed her the letter and she went on to read about the presentation dinner in London.

It was a national competition open to catering students

and professional caterers. A few weeks before we were due to take our finals at college one of the tutors had asked us to enter the competition. Rather reluctantly we did. A fortnight later we all received a pen through the post with compliments of Lever Industrial. A subtle way of saying that you haven't come anywhere, I thought. Two months later I realised my thoughts were wrong! I was over-whelmed and so was my tutor.

It was a marvellous end to the very special time in Limpsfield.

14

In captivity

She cannot escape
From bars in the cage,
Shut in for hours
Her mind in a rage.

Her heart is cold
And emotions none,
She tries to be bold
But life's no fun.

She dreams each day
Of hills and mountains,
How she'd fly away
Towards crystal fountains.

The world outside
Is bright and gay
Like a leaping tide
Is how she should stay.

Not a dark drab room
Cold and bare,
Full of gloom
But open in the air.

Fly to the place
I've loved so long,
Soar up with grace
And sing my song.

Let me live and love
And be free to do
Like any other dove
What she wishes to.

I was filled with happiness: life was so exciting, there was such a lot to learn, so much to explore. The first Sunday back at home I had arranged to meet Sue's sister, Helen, who lived quite near me. She was going to introduce me to Greyfriars church, which she attended. We went along to both the morning and evening services and she then introduced me to Crossroads, the young people's group who meet to sing, pray and discuss. There was a lovely atmosphere and I knew that I had found something very special. Afterwards I was offered a lift home. I found myself squashed up in the back of a mini with another girl, a guitar across our laps pinning us firmly to the seat. Tania introduced herself and somehow we got on to the subject of hospitals, to discover that we had been in the same one. She went on to explain how she had to have an operation on her arm after a cycling accident.

"What were you in the Royal Berks for?" she asked.

"Anorexia," I replied.

She put her hand out to mine and shook it. "Snap!"

God certainly moves in a mysterious way. The friend which Nicky had prayed that I would find was pinned to the back seat of a mini with me. I could not have found a more ideal friend if I had tried; a Christian who had beaten anorexia! What more could I have wanted? We exchanged addresses and arranged to meet the next day.

The following day we sat talking over a cup of coffee. Firstly, we enlightened each other on what we were doing: she was taking A-levels at school and wanted to go on to read medicine at university. Then our conversation turned to the inevitable – anorexia. She asked me about my experiences and how I felt now. It was so encouraging to talk to someone who had come through the illness. My anguish was once hers and she knew only too well what I was talking about. She went on to ask me how important a part my faith played in my recovery and posed a question which made me think very deeply about the situation.

"Do you want Jesus as your hero?"

"Yes, I do," I replied.

"What you do to your body you are doing to Jesus'. If you love Him and really want Him, then He will live in you and be a part of you, but by not eating the right things you hurt Him as much as you damage yourself."

What she said was very true. I realised what she was getting at, that if I loved Jesus with all my heart how could I hurt Him by damaging myself? I understood how to overcome the psychological side of anorexia – mind over matter – but what about the physical side? How does one overcome not being hungry, revulsion at the sight of food, and nausea?

"Jesus died to save us suffering," Tania explained. "Our agony is His; He bears our burdens. In other words He can take from us our fears and illnesses if only we are prepared to let Him help us. We should be living our lives in glory for God. We cannot do that if we are heavily laden with fear."

I realised that there are three dimensions to overcoming anorexia: physical, psychological and spiritual. The one dimension that I had neglected was the spiritual – the most important of all. As Tania said, "Jesus can take from us our fears and illnesses."

A few days later Tania came round to my house after school. We had hardly known each other, yet we had so much to say and so much to share. She asked if she could read some of my poetry. I handed her a selection. There was silence. She looked up at me from where she was sitting cross-legged on the floor.

"I've never been moved to tears by poetry before."

She picked up one of my latest poems. "You really are in captivity aren't you?"

I had not realised that the poem reflected my feelings so

much. My agony of feeling trapped in anorexia was portrayed through the agony of a captive dove.

Tania mentioned that she had been very much helped by a doctor in Oxford and that I ought to make an appointment to see him.

"It may seem a long way to go, but I am sure you'd travel to Timbuctoo (whoever he is) to get better. When I had it, I certainly did."

I told her I did not consider myself sufficiently ill to see a doctor.

"You might think that you're better physically, but I can tell you that psychologically you're nowhere near cured. Please get in touch with Doctor P.J. He's a miracle worker!"

She later sent me two passages from the Bible to look up:

He helps us in all our troubles, so that we are able to help others who have all kinds of troubles, using the same help that we ourselves have received from God (2 Cor. 1:4).

"Keep up the good work!" she added.

Happy is the person who remains faithful under trials, because when he succeeds in passing such a test, he will receive as his reward the life which God has promised to those who love him (Jas. 1:12).

She finished, "Well! I've been through it; I pray I can help you Helena."

At first, I couldn't find the motivation to contact the doctor. Yet deep down I knew anorexia still had a hold on my life.

I was struggling with a psychological battle. I was on the defensive with people, and felt as though the world hated me. This feeling of being hated did not turn into rejection, but a need to search to understand the meaning of life. In my need I turned to the Bible for reassurance.

If the world hates you just remember that it has hated me
first. If you belonged to the world, then the world would
love you as its own. But I chose you from this world, and
you do not belong to it; that is why the world hates you
(John 15: 18–19).

One night I felt so dispirited that I decided to ring Tania
and ask if I could go over and talk to her. We chatted for a
couple of hours drinking endless cups of tea. We talked
about both serious and crazy things; we laughed and
almost cried. Throughout the evening the pain in the
bones of my legs increased, becoming agonising. If only
the whole illness could be behind me, I thought. I looked
at Tania, full of life, full of praise for how wonderful life
is.

"When I had anorexia," she said, "life was terrible and I
was so boring. Look at me now – Well, maybe don't! I can
really enjoy life, it's such fun."

I glanced at her enviously as I noticed the difference
between us.

"Don't you want to enjoy life again, Helena?"

I sighed heavily. "Yes! I do."

"Let's go and phone Doctor P.J. now," she said.

I sat and waited whilst Tania spoke to him. Everything
was arranged: all I had to do was to ring up the following
day to make an appointment with him.

Then the moment of truth came, the initial consultation with Doctor P.J. He saw my parents and me
together first to establish the background of my illness and
their reactions to it. Then he spent quite a long time
discussing the problem with me alone. He asked how I felt
now, about my eating patterns and my attitude towards
my body and weight.

Then he suggested that I was weighed. I dreaded the
thought; I had avoided weighing myself for over a year. He
asked how much I thought I weighed. I said about seven
and a half stone; it was a wild guess and wishful thinking.
I stood on the scales. My weight was over the figure of

eight stone of which I had lived in fear for the past five years. The thought repulsed me. Even if I was a little under the average weight for my height of five feet five and a half inches and age of nineteen, it was only a matter of pounds and I felt terrible.

The main thing that Doctor P.J. was concerned about was that I had at last faced reality. Nevertheless, I left the consultation feeling very disheartened.

I was to see him once a month for an hour, when we would work through the problem together. In the short time that I had spoken to him I knew that I had come to the right person. He was realistic and concerned not only with treating the illness, but healing the person as a whole, which I think is essential in a psychosomatic disease.

A couple of weeks later I was asked if I could return to St George's House in Windsor Castle for about a month, as one of the cooks was ill. This time I stayed with my godparents as opposed to sharing the flat with the other cook. However, for the first two nights I slept in one of the guest rooms in St George's House. After I had finished work on the second day I had a sudden severe attack of depression. In my desperation I fled home. My father had quite a shock when driving back from work he saw me wandering along in the dark from the bus stop. He stopped the car and I climbed in. He said that my cousin, Kathie, had phoned from Bermuda last night to remind us of her brother's television programme being shown the following night. I was feeling so low that I decided to phone her back. She suggested I arranged to go over there again. I planned to go out just after Christmas. It was something super to look forward to. I stayed at home that night and got up early in the morning to go back to Windsor.

I enjoyed the remaining weeks at St George's House. It was less exhausting than last time and we had some interesting people to cook for. Partway through the month I had my second appointment with Doctor P.J. The two aspects which seemed to come out most strongly

were self-consciousness and self-acceptance. The conversation began with anxiety and how it affected my eating
patterns. On the whole, when I was anxious or worried I
lost my appetite and stopped eating. This led on to
assessing the kind of mood I was in when I binged, why it
happened and how I felt afterwards. I explained my
feelings of guilt and revulsion. He told me that purging
would not alter my weight because the food had already
been absorbed. It had a purely psychological effect of
relieving my guilt and in fact could have drastic effects on
my body and disrupt the use of my colon and rectum. I was
aware of the effects that it was having on my body, but
until such a time that I could establish sensible eating
patterns I could see no end to it.

From eating we went on to talk about weight, size, shape
and general appearance, discussing the parts of me about
which I was self-conscious – my hips and thighs. Doctor
P.J. said that he could tell that it was that area of my body
because of the way in which I hid it underneath big
jumpers. I then had to explain my feelings and reactions if
I was forced to wear very light clothes. I did this with
tremendous difficulty. It was not easy to make such an
attempt because it meant facing reality. Whatever I said it
always seemed to indicate my inability to accept myself or
face reality. My weight had not changed from the previous
month.

The time passed so quickly that before I realised it I had
finished working at Windsor. I returned home to complete
a few Christmas cakes which I had on order and to work on
a correspondence course which I was taking. After a few
days I felt extremely tired and had sharp pains in my head.
In the middle of the night I woke up with a fever and an
excruciating pain across my stomach. My parents called
the doctor who said it was a gastro-intestinal virus and
gave me some pain killers, but I could not stop being sick,
so he came back and gave me something to ease it. Not
surprisingly I lost a little weight. However, the fact that I
did not continue to lose weight after the virus had gone

showed that I was definitely on the road to recovery from anorexia nervosa.

We had a lovely family Christmas and three days afterwards I flew out to Bermuda for five weeks. Peter, Joy and Kathie were at the airport to meet me. As we drove from St Davids, the island on which the airport is situated, across the causeway and on towards Hamilton, the capital of Bermuda, I was filled with exhilaration. I knew that there was a reason for my coming back to this tiny island in the middle of the Atlantic, and it was far greater than having a holiday and capturing sub-tropical beauties.

The island was more breathtakingly beautiful than I remembered, with its attractively designed houses in a range of pastel colours all capped with their white limestone roofs, and gardens a mass of luscious citrus trees and banana plants heavily laden with fruit – a flame of colour. Palm trees gracefully reach towards the skyline; hedgerows overflow with rich pink hibiscus flowers; the island abounds in deep red poinsettias, contrasting with the spiky green leaves of the spanish bayonets. The collection of pink sandy beaches; healthy vegetation extending to the beaches' edge and the turquoise blue sea lapping on to its shore; the volcanic rock which juts out of the water in irregular shapes, with fascinating sea-creatures clinging to its sides; the crystal-clear blue sea, which is purple over the coral reefs, filled with a vast selection of fish, including barracuda, yellowtail snappers, wahoe, Bermuda chub, rainbow runners and parrot fish, along with some incredible coral formations and wonderful underwater creations are a world of their own.

The atmosphere was one, very much, of festivity, with Gombey dancers in their multi-coloured costumes performing in the streets, the New Year to see in, not to mention the numerous invitations to "open house" parties. However enjoyable such times were, I benefited most through simply talking to Kathie. Discussing past situations and consequent pain gave me the opportunity to look at the past objectively and give thought to relationships, in particular between my immediate family. It enabled me to put the pieces of the puzzle together, to comprehend some of the difficulties, past and present, and where possible to amend the situation.

It seemed obvious that my parents had had problems in their marriage, to a greater or lesser degree, from very early days. Moving to Kenya immediately after they married created difficulties for my mother who was not accustomed to the Kenyan way of life, did not find it easy to live on a research station, nor knew how to spend the hours of such empty days. Then having two children was not the bed of roses perhaps she had hoped it to be – especially when I came along! Moving to England was a strain for the whole family, in particular for my father who left behind a good job and a country he loved. When after a matter of months we found somewhere to live and he had another job, I know it did not match the work he had enjoyed so much in Africa.

Whilst Ruth and I were still quite young my mother used to get extremely tired and would often have to crawl up the stairs to put us both to bed. Undoubtedly her state at such times did not ease their relationship. Other than such incidents, I think they shared a happy marriage. Any other conflicts were probably due to very differing personalities: my father hides his feelings and appears cool, calm and collected and buries problems by becoming involved in work; my mother is far more emotional and brings problems out into the open.

Until my teenage years I shared a very good relationship with both my parents. Not uncommonly, problems began around this age, firstly with my father who made me feel extremely uncomfortable and from whom I distanced myself. Then with my mother who appeared to possess me and who I felt was "moulding" me. It left me feeling trapped and frustrated, unable to express myself, unable to be myself without feeling a take-over bid. In the last year the difficulties encountered with my father had escalated. After much discussion and thought I realised why I felt so uneasy with him; I was seeing the wrong side of him. Over the years his true self had been suppressed. Underneath lay vivacity, adventure, appreciation of beauty, fun and wit. When I got home I tried to bring out this side of him and discard the false image which had been cast. I began to see a different person altogether and I now get on extremely well with him.

I realised that my difficulties with my mother were far more complex; not only did it require my breaking away but her letting go, treating me as an individual and not a part of herself. This was to result in a certain amount of argument, which was no bad thing because it cleaned the system, but caused considerable inner conflict for me and, I imagine, heartache for her.

The terrible relationship I had with Ruth was perhaps inevitable, but on the other hand, perhaps some of our suffering could have been prevented. Talking to Kathie about how I felt during these times acted as a therapy, bringing to the surface hidden feelings of rejection and resentment. I started to put such feelings into the past. This enabled me, at a later date, to begin to discuss with Ruth how she felt during those years, in the hope that a better understanding of each other would develop. We now share a good relationship, even if there is a lot of healing to be done.

With my new awareness of relationships and past events, I spent the last few days in Bermuda soaking up the sun in picturesque surroundings, thinking about the question Tania had asked me, "Don't you want to enjoy life again, Helena?" For the first time I *really* wanted to take hold of that "good life" she spoke of.

15

Invisible strength

That deep piercing pain
Which burrows into my heart
And dwells in all my body,
Suddenly begins to part.

The intensity is fading
And beauty is intertwined;
An ever growing love
Calms my restless mind.

How can I explain
This incredible feeling,
When an invisible strength
Gives peace to my whole being.

I need not explain why,
Just let the peace flow through
Know that God is here
And thank Him in all I do.

Helped by the Bermudan sunshine, winter passed quickly back in England and the first sign of spring brought with it new life. Quite by chance I decided to go to the Women's World Day of Prayer. I know I was led there, if only to hear what Joyce, the speaker, had to say.

She began by describing how we might let God into one room only of our being.

"After release in the spirit," she went on, "it is as if Our Lord says, 'I know I am welcome here in this room, but I desire to be Lord of all your house.' Panic usually seizes one! One thinks of the rest of the house and the disorder and dismay in the different rooms. However, Jesus says, 'Do not be afraid, take my hand and we shall go through your house together.' He then says, 'We shall start with the attic.' This is usually a most disconcerting suggestion and maybe we remonstrate with Jesus, and say, politely of course, 'But Lord, there is so much rubbish and junk up there.' 'Yes, I know,' says Jesus, 'but take my hand and we shall go together. I quite agree there is junk and we will discard this together, but also there are precious things up there that you do not know about, which I desire for you to use for me in My Kingdom.'

"Jesus continues, 'After the attic, may I go into your bedroom – this is the room where images are set in place, where masks are carefully put on. Maybe relationships are not in My order in this room – do not fear I am the answer to all problems.' He says, 'I will teach you to remove your mask and show you that I love and accept you unconditionally, just as you are, and also teach you to love and accept yourself unconditionally, because I do.' He asks, 'May we go into your kitchen, and may I sit in the corner and listen to all the conversation? May I hear the

loving things you say about your family, to your family,
and about your neighbours and friends? May I listen to
you as you upbuild my body?' He then asks, 'Do you have a
basement?' We truly shudder. 'Do not be afraid of the
basement in your life – your hidden past, maybe guilt,
resentment, fear, anxiety . . . even dark corners that have no
name – do not be afraid. I am the Light of the World and I
have taken you out of the darkness. Come, let me heal all
the wounds of your past as I have promised to bind up all
wounds. Will you invite me to be Lord of every room in
your life?'"

On my way home and during the rest of the week I went
over and over Joyce's address. I thought back to the time of
Limpsfield when I opened my "door" wide and welcomed
God in; how wonderfully happy I felt then, and how glad I
was that I had really accepted Him. It seemed amazing that
Jesus had taken my hand and was gently leading me
through the different rooms. He had already started work
in my attic, discarding the rubbish and bringing out the
precious things which He desires I use for Him. He had
shown me that relationships were not in His order. Above
all, He had given me the most fantastic reassurance, that
He loved and accepted me unconditionally and He was
also teaching me to love and accept myself – something I
could never do in the past. Jesus had moved through so
many rooms, tidying, cleaning and polishing them; it was
marvellous the work He was doing and I really wanted
Him to be Lord of my life. I recalled the question at the end
of the address, "Will you invite me to be Lord of every
room in your life?" "No! Not my basement," I thought. "I
have hidden the key. No one enters my basement; it is filled
with dark corners and buried pain."

At the end of the week Tania rang me up to see if I would
like to go to the service at Greyfriars church on Sunday and
then on to Crossroads (the young people's group). It had
been over three months since I had gone and although I
liked the church and had received a very warm welcome, I
had never felt a part of it. Nevertheless I decided it would
be nice to go along.

I was overwhelmed when I heard Ian's talk at Crossroads; it followed exactly Joyce's address at the Women's World Day of Prayer. He spoke about the importance of giving God the key to every room in our house, and my mind was immediately transported to the hidden key of my basement. Ian went on to stress that if we really love God, we must not only give all our keys but give up our old lives and start anew. This can be fulfilled by letting God's Holy Spirit come into us. Could God be trying to tell me something? I thought. It was certainly more than chance that I had attended both meetings. Perhaps God was trying to say that not until I revealed my basement could I be completely cured of anorexia and that through revealing it my faith would grow. In many ways I wanted to speak to Ian about not being able to hand over my basement to God but I did not have the courage.

At that moment, Joan, the vicar's wife and a Crossroads' leader, came over and said how nice it was to see me again. I appreciated her warm welcome and felt encouraged.

That night I spent several hours considering what to do about my hidden memories and pain. I very much needed to bring them out into the open and I knew that until I had done this, I could not be fully cured of anorexia, but the thought of facing those dark corners alone was more than I could bear.

The following afternoon I plucked up courage and decided to go and see Joan. I explained my difficulties and was soon convinced that I had done the right thing in coming. I began to realise that I would not be facing the dark corners alone – Jesus would be beside me in every move I made. I longed for Him to come and walk with me, but I was scared that in handing over my anorexia I would lose self-control; have no control over my body and myself.

Joan explained that God does not take our self-control from us. We still have control over what we do: God merely offers us an alternative and is there to guide us.

When I arrived home I decided to look up the passage in the Bible which Ian had mentioned at the end of his talk: "But the Spirit produces love, joy, peace, patience, kindness, goodness, faithfulness, humility and self-control (Gal. 5:22–3)." I leapt with joy when I read the last two words: No, God doesn't take self-control from us; He gives it to us!

The next Sunday at church we sang one of my favourite hymns, "My song is love unknown." The words touched me deeply and I felt particularly close to God, yet for some reason I left the church feeling empty and down. I knew that I had to talk and pray with Ian as Joan had previously suggested. When I arrived the sky was dark and oppressive and as we discussed the problem the rain fell in heavy sheets. Ian said that he felt my past feelings of rejection, my depressions and anorexia were closely linked and that he would like to pray, with his wife, that I would be released from these things and filled with God's Spirit. I felt happy about their praying for me and afterwards felt warm and tranquil.

I was still having regular consultations with Doctor P.J. in Oxford, and each time I saw him after returning from Bermuda he noticed a change for the better in me. When I visited him in March, after talking with Ian, he suggested there should be a longer gap between this and my next consultation, which in fact proved to be my last. The one thing which seemed to come across most strongly to him was the fact that I was now beginning to face reality. The weeks in Bermuda had given me the opportunity to be myself and more and more I realised the importance of this. I think it is a very difficult task to fulfil because it involves self-acceptance, looking at one's life objectively, being open and unafraid and in the long run, facing reality. It is far easier to project a false image which is aesthetically pleasing, but in doing this we are not true to ourselves and the effect is inner frustration.

Two people confirmed the importance of this matter. My friend Doris wrote:

I think you have a most interesting life ahead of you, giving so much of which you have an abundance –

sensitivity, experience and artistic talent. I am quite serious about this: just go on being yourself, and having the courage to be yourself. So many people feel that they have to project the image that has been cast for them by family and tradition. I'm not decrying the latter for they have helped to create the person, but to try to express oneself within these confines can be frustrating.

Kathie also told me:

Nobody can destroy *you*: you are who you are, and whatever you do or touch, your stamp is on that. What media you choose to express yourself is *not* important; what is important is that you are true to yourself in that form of expression.

The fear of letting anorexia go had disappeared and I began to realise that my complete recovery and freedom would be as a result of a process, a journey.

Love was the first thing I had to comprehend. I had spent my time searching for love and security in the things I did, and more especially in the people I met. My endless searching was to no avail. Then, one day, I was thumbing through my Bible haphazardly and three words leapt out at me from 1 John chapter 4: "God is love." "God is love," I repeated to myself, "Wow! I've discovered love."

I went on to read: "Whoever loves is a child of God and knows God. Whoever does not love does not know God, for God is love. And God showed his love for us by sending his only Son into the world, so that we might have life through him. This is what love is: it is not that we have loved God, but that he loved us and sent his Son to be the means by which our sins are forgiven" (1 John 4:7–10).

I knew that I had found something extremely precious; not only the meaning of love, but a love which would *never* let me down, because it was not my love, but God's love for me.

From love, my journey led me to loneliness. Through

the fear of loneliness and through the agony of its grip I could not see a solution. I have no control over it, but surely God does, I thought to myself. God would help me to overcome my feelings of loneliness. My prayers were not answered.

Suddenly I realised that it was the *fear* of loneliness that I should be praying for, not loneliness itself, because there had to be a reason for my suffering. I turned to the Bible for an explanation. There in Isaiah I found this passage.

> Do not be afraid – I am with you!
> I am your God – let nothing terrify you!
> I will make you strong and help you:
> I will protect you and save you.

> (Isa. 41:10)

God did not take my loneliness from me, but He removed the fears and showed me that something very special would develop through my suffering these feelings. As it says in 2 Corinthians, "For when I am weak, then I am strong."

My fear of loneliness had gone but I still held my fear of the uncertainty of the future. It took a long time for this to be released because I could not grasp the fact that the future should be in God's hands not mine. But my worries over what the future held and the many failed plans disappeared when I handed it all over to God. I read a passage in the Psalms which told me, "The Lord says, 'I will teach you the way you should go; I will instruct you and advise you.'"

"Okay Lord," I said, "It's in *your* hands; do what you will."

I don't know if He took that as a challenge but He certainly had some dramatic, surprising and exciting happenings in store for me!

The hardest stage in my journey was overcoming past pain and not letting it affect the present or the future, and also, totally forgiving the people who had caused me anguish. I had to relive much of the pain in order for it to be released from my body and for the memories no longer to hurt.

I was particularly close to God during this part of my journey and He was very good to me, restoring my self-confidence, forgiving my sins, leading and upholding me, but there were times when He seemed distant and I could not reach Him. On one such occasion I went over to Greyfriars church to see Joan. Her understanding of the situation helped me enormously.

"You're on a bumpy road and God is the only one who can make it straight. You have to ask Him to guide you over the bumps and to enter into the worst places with you in order that the hills may gradually become flat."

I realised where I had gone wrong: I was not putting *all* my trust in God. I thought of that wonderful verse in James: "But when you pray, you must believe and not doubt at all. Whoever doubts is like a wave in the sea that is driven and blown about by the wind" (Jas. 1:6).

Joan went on to talk about the importance of prayer in healing past pain, and of putting everything before God's judgment and not our own. She read a passage from the Bible: "Trust in the Lord with all your heart. Never rely on what you think you know. Remember the Lord in everything you do, and he will show you the right way. Never let yourself think that you are wiser than you are; simply obey the Lord and refuse to do wrong. If you do, it will be like good medicine, healing your wounds and easing your pains."

I went home feeling reassured and with the knowledge that much prayer was needed. I brought all my troubles before God and asked that He would forgive my sins. A tranquillity filled my body and mind as I lay in the understanding that all around me was God, next to me was Jesus and inside me was the Holy Spirit. Yet there was no division between them; they were three in one. I asked God to show me a verse in the Bible. It read:

I have swept your sins away like a cloud.
Come back to me; I am the one who saves you.

(Isa. 44:22)

When I awoke the next morning I had a strange sensation
of having been re-created. I felt different, calmed and filled
with happiness. I felt differently towards God: I was far
more aware of His presence, of my love for Him and my
utter dependence on Him. Even the world appeared to
have changed: I saw a new beauty in nature, the delicate
flowers, graceful trees, the brilliant rays of the sun and
dramatic formation of the sky. As I walked outside to hear
the melodious singing of the birds, smell the sweet
perfume of the multi-coloured blossom and see the
wonderful array of greenery, I had a compulsive desire to
express my feelings through poetry and art. This resulted
in a burst of creativity.

While I was spending much of my time painting for
pleasure it was decided that Greyfriars church needed a
mural done. It was for one of the rooms being converted
into a meeting place and coffee bar for the unemployed, to
be known as the Daybreak Centre. Members of Crossroads
were asked to submit designs if they were interested.
Claire's picture, simple and incorporating the word
'Daybreak', was chosen for the main wall, but as she had
sent it in anonymously I was asked to paint the mural. My
own submission, along with another girl's, would be used
for smaller panels across the room.

One afternoon when I was balancing on the top of a
ladder with paint dribbling down my arm, a man walked
into the room who was to play an important part in the
next stage of my life. As we talked, I discovered that he was
the administrator of the new Greyfriars Centre which
houses a sports hall and various smaller rooms, including
a book and craft shop and a coffee lounge. John and I
started to discuss writing and art, and on hearing that I
was writing a book about my experience with anorexia
which had been accepted for publication, he suggested the

possibility of a promotion day at the Centre. He also expressed interest in my design for the Daybreak Centre and asked whether I had given any thought to getting it printed.

At a later date when John and I had been able to talk at greater length, all the possibilities seemed to come together. As I started to develop my painting, he suggested that I use the Centre to exhibit and sell my work. This was a real incentive and inspiration and I found it exciting that so many good things were arising from the gift of my time in the painting of that mural.

Shortly after the mural had been completed, I went with Crossroads for a camping weekend on a farm near Andover. I benefited a great deal from these few days, which held some very precious moments, and looking back I realise that there were two main reasons for my being there: to enable me to become more open and to gain a new insight into suffering.

We arrived on the Friday evening to find ourselves in the most beautifully peaceful surroundings. The girls' tents, sleeping about six people each, were pitched in the farmhouse garden. The boys' tents shared a field with the cows! Our meeting place was a large and exceptionally well-equipped barn. Besides a collection of straw bales on which to sit, there was a long wooden table at which the whole group could be seated for meals, several skittle alleys, a sink and electrical points which were used for the kettle and electric piano. It was here that we met each morning and evening to sing, pray and listen to the talks.

It was an opportunity to get to know the other members of Crossroads far better. In the wonderfully relaxed atmosphere I really began to feel a part of the group and valued as one of its members. I became less introverted and my past feelings of not belonging completely disappeared.

The leaders exhausted us mentally, cramming a great many of the teachings of the Bible into a very short time, and also succeeded in exhausting us physically. Under the brilliant beams of the sun, during what must have been one of England's hottest summers, we played rounders, cricket and football, among numerous other activities.

The talks given throughout the weekend were based on the letter of James in the New Testament. The letter begins by talking about suffering and it was this section which had an incredible impact on me and left me deep in thought for the rest of the camp and many weeks after.

My brothers consider yourselves fortunate when all kinds of trials come your way (Jas. 1:2).

James was telling us to consider ourselves fortunate in times of trial which seemed crazy until I realised the explanation which followed:

for you know that when your faith succeeds in facing such trials, the result is the ability to endure (Jas. 1:3).

I saw that it is not the suffering itself we should consider fortunate to have, but the good which comes out of our ability to face the suffering. James then goes on to tell us:

Make sure that your endurance carries you all the way without failing, so that you may be perfect and complete, lacking nothing.

It appears that James is stressing the utmost importance of battling with our trials until the very end, for only then will we gain from our suffering.

My past attitude towards suffering had been one of fear and resentment, compared with the attitude we are told to have in the Bible, one of rejoicing. I realised through a verse in Peter that not only should we accept and be glad about our suffering but, in order for it to be used for good, we must put our complete trust in God.

So then, those who suffer because it is God's will for them, should by their good actions trust themselves completely to their Creator, who always keeps his promise (1 Pet. 4:19).

Peter also looked at suffering in the most wonderful way as a privilege.

> My dear friends, do not be surprised at the painful test you are suffering, as though something unusual were happening to you. Rather be glad that you are sharing Christ's sufferings, so that you may be full of joy when his glory is revealed. (1 Pet. 4:12–13).

When I read St Paul's letter to the Romans at a later date he also seemed to speak of suffering as a privilege.

> Since we are his children, we will possess the blessings he keeps for his people, and we will also possess with Christ what God has kept for him; for if we share Christ's suffering, we will also share his glory. I consider that what we suffer at this present time cannot be compared at all with the glory that is going to be revealed to us. (Rom. 8:17–18).

This concept became more and more amazing to me and I found myself actually thanking God for all that had happened over the years because I began to see the marvellous way in which He was beginning to use it. This, along with a verse I recently found in Peter, gave me the strength to face times of trial and gain from them.

> God will bless you for this, if you endure the pain of undeserved suffering because you are conscious of his will. (1 Pet. 2:19).

I returned home with the knowledge that a new life lay ahead of me. I felt excited at the prospects before me of developing a career using art, dance and writing. Along with this, came the need to become more independent and

I took the opportunity to move to a flat nearer to the centre in Reading.

Although so much joy and hope was coming into my life I was well aware that we cannot for ever remain on the mountain top and that life has its difficulties. I see this as a spiritual battle of love and joy against despair and desperation; a realisation that we have to fight for true life, but that fight will not be beyond our strength, as it says in 1 Corinthians:

> But God keeps his promise, and he will not allow you to be tested beyond your power to remain firm; at the time you are put to the test, he will give you the strength to endure it, and so provide you with a way out. (10:13).

I saw through a verse which Joan gave me that it is not only the strength God gives us but inner tranquillity as we know His love.

> The Lord your God is with you
> He is mighty to save.
> He will take great delight in you,
> He will quiet you with His love,
> He will rejoice over you with singing.
>
> (Zeph. 3:17 NIV)

With all these things behind me, at nineteen, I find great beauty and comfort in the words from Isaiah:

> But the Lord says,
> 'Do not cling to events of the past
>   or dwell on what happened long ago.
> Watch for the new thing I am going
>   to do.
>   It is happening already – you can see
>   it now!
> I will make a road through the
>   wilderness
> and give you streams of water there.'
>
> (Isa. 43:18–19)